# UNHINDERED BY FEAR

By Esther Marie

UNHINDERED BY FEAR by Esther Marie
info@fearlessco.org

ISBN: 9781713294429

Cover and Illustrations: Leslie Moreno Editor: Eve
Gualtieri
Fearless Co. www.fearlessco.org

# We help you win against fear so  your dreams can have a chance to live.

FEARLESS CO.

# GRATITUDE

I want to thank my entire family for their love & support, especially my Uncle Vince, whom I told I would write a book about overcoming fears one Thanksgiving several years ago while scooping mashed potatoes onto my plate. Couldn't let him down, so I did it.

**UNHINDERED BY FEAR**

# CONTENTS

# AN
# INTRODUCTION

The first edition of this book was released two years ago and had a tremendous impact on the lives of women struggling with fear, anxiety, and depression (though this second edition has been written to impact both men and women). My friend Ebie Hepworth, who had recently joined me as a co-leader of a company I founded, co-wrote the book with me. That company was called Fearless Girl and had a mission to reach girls with a message of hope using the concept of adventure and action sports to tell our stories. We were extremely involved in the surf community in Orange County, California and raised awareness about Human Trafficking through partnered organizations. Since then, Fearless Girl has evolved into what is now Fearless Co., a content-based creative studio producing powerful content to engage in conversation and see radical change. Our media

9

resources are designed to inspire individuals to reshape their thinking, bring freedom from their internal battles and initiate a shift in our culture. We tackle topics surrounding fear and encourage an authentic community within our following.

When Ebie and I first wrote this book, we were two young zealous souls with a level of ambition even Kanye himself couldn't keep up with. Ebie and her husband Zac were in the process of adopting their two children from Liberia and I had just applied to go back to school and finish my degree in Ministerial Leadership. Ebie was working for a non-profit while fundraising, selling all her furniture to pay for the adoption, staying up late hours to make macrame decor, quilting for her future babies and only God knows what else. I was working three jobs (literally was a catering director, managed a pillowcase business in some lady's garage and nannied enough kids to populate a nation) to help fund the production of our book and E-course that would coincide with the book. Not only did we set out to write a book (and complete it in 3 months), but we also committed to rebrand Fearless Girl. We gathered our closest friends and filmed the E-course along a six-day road trip throughout California, while simultaneously pulling off a Kickstarter campaign that helped us raise over five thousand dollars to finish the projects. As if that wasn't enough, Zac and Ebie were traveling between Boise and the Philippines with the non-profit they worked for so facetime became our boardroom for business meetings. On occasion, I'd get a text from Ebie saying she'd be in town for a random gig they were getting paid for. So we'd meet at the Disneyland hotel, stretch out on the Mickey Mouse carpet and dream, plot and strategize into Fearless Co. (I'm telling you there's magic in that carpet)!

Needless to say, we poured our hearts into the first edition of this book. We have been so blessed by the messages and testimonies of girls who have found freedom, confidence and joy after reading the words imprinted on these pages. However, as the years have gone by we have grown so much both personally and as an organization. Ebie has recently transitioned out of Fearless Co. as an active member, but sits on the board of advisors and celebrates the freedom that continues to pour out of this organization. Though her contributions to this book have been omitted, her prayers, wisdom, and love remain. In this second edition reprint, the content has been updated to build upon the initial message we introduced two years ago. We've renamed the book Unhindered By Fear to challenge our community (and ourselves) to dig deep into what it means to live fearlessly. With a name like Fearless Co., the word 'fearless' can become redundant, rhetorical and lose it's meaning. The last thing we want is to become a trend in our community and lose sight of our mission. We are committed to calling out the bull crap on the fear that holds us back from living transparent lives and being fully connected to our true identity.

Ebie and I pray you will feel revived by hope, like oxygen being breathed into your lungs, as you read the words declared over you in these pages. The past two years have taught us to cling to faith in the midst of the darkest valleys, chaotic storms and most depressing nights and believe the light will shine again. Fear is a heck of a liar, but the good news is that eventually those lies run out of breath and if you anchor yourself to truth, you will outlast the lie. I hope you're ready to start living, cause good things await!

# UNHINDERED BY FEAR

# GET THE [F]ear
# OUT OF YOUR HEAD

That's right, fear lives in the little six-inch space between your ears and receives far more fanfare than it deserves. You've been a hospitable host to fear, tolerating its' unwelcome presence, changing your plans, dragging your feet, uncertain of commitments and wasting more energy entertaining your doubts than pursuing your dreams. Anxiety is your new normal and you've found comfort in holding back, hiding out and self-protecting. It makes sense though, right? I mean, vulnerability? That's scary! Having hope? You're just asking to be disappointed! The voice of fear echoes in your head like your favorite Spotify playlist on repeat. However, you would never recognize this voice as your enemy, because it's disguised as your best friend, even

13

in its most condemning and accusatory tone, you encourage it and even seek it out. This voice drills you with a never-ending list of necessary self-improvement tasks you must complete in order to achieve perfection and be worth loving. It incites confusion by insistent questions about your past or your future, strategically distracting you from the present. Fear is like a disease, covered up by symptoms of issues that arise in our lives. Many of the symptoms that we deal with distract us from dealing with the main issue, which is fear itself. You may struggle with insecurity, intimidation, disappointment, or discouragement, to name a few. But all of these issues are symptoms of the root cause of fear.

Many people will tell you that positive thinking and positive living is the best way to alleviate stress and anxiety. And while having a positive outlook on life is helpful, it deflects from the main source of pain. Stress and anxiety are rooted in fears and disguised as a surface level issue so you live in a constant state of confusion and eventually give up looking for a cure. Fear loves to control, and unfortunately, we live in a world where people use fear to manipulate our finances, emotions and decision making. Living free from fear gives you the freedom to live confidently and regain control of your life. Here's the good news: it doesn't need to take a lifetime. You can learn today how to confront your fear at the root; get the [F]ear out of your head and start living. The play on words is intentional as we have discovered that most people are living in their fantasy life inside their head just as much as they are living in fear. You may not struggle with negative thoughts. Instead, your personal battle may be finding the confidence to make a shift in your career, lose weight and get healthy, allow a relationship to blossom, or whatever it may be. You have a positive hope for the future, but because you are afraid of letting go of what you currently have, you live in your head and fantasize about what it would be like, yet never make moves to make it happen. Fear is taking up space in your head and therefore robbing you of the courage to achieve your dreams. Well, we've had enough of that. Hang tight, we're going to get you to a better place!

As we shared in the introduction, we have created a tool to help break down this concept using the captivating imagery of adventure. Adventure alone does not have the power to heal, restore, or bring freedom. We live in a culture where many young people are drawn to wander, live a remote lifestyle and travel the world in pursuit of ultimate freedom. While this is a compelling lifestyle, it is a short-lived experience that leads to a non-committal emotional experience. Don't get us wrong, we are huge advocates for adventure! Surfing is exhilarating, climbing mountains is a rush and sometimes there's nothing I'd rather do than sell everything, live in a Volkswagen bus and eat Ramen noodles every night. And perhaps there is a season in life that this experience is beneficial and empowering. However, these pursuits on their own leave us empty and searching for more. Humanity longs for satisfaction and when we don't find it in our jobs, relationships, partying, addictive behaviors or money, we go bury our lives in obsessive pleasures to distract us from what we truly desire: purpose.

There is only one antidote to the endless search for more: having faith. It's the thing that propels you into living the most wild and free adventure you could ever imagine. This discovery is essential to life, it's essential to humanity and it's essential to becoming truly unhindered by fear. Maybe you've attempted this whole "having faith" thing before and decided it's not for you or just doesn't work. Before you put this book back on the shelf because you didn't realize it was going to be "religious"- I ask you to WAIT! Don't judge a book by it's cover...or actually maybe you should because the cover of this book is pretty epic! Keep reading and have an open mind. What are you afraid of? After all, isn't that why you started reading this book? Are you struggling with anxiety, insecurity, doubt, depression, OCD, or another kind of fear? If so, that's no way to go through life, full of limits. We're here to accompany you along a journey to tackling those fears head-on. We have come up with an easy to understand illustration to equip you in becoming fearless. It's not a secret magic sauce (unfortunately, otherwise we'd smother that goodness all over our tacos). Instead, this illustration serves as a guide- a map, like you would get upon entering your favorite national park. I have a map of Yosemite National Park sitting in my glove compartment of my car right now. But just because I have that map doesn't mean I'm an expert at navigating Yosemite. I have to first study the map, explore each path, discover the best route, and set my feet on the terrain to begin the journey. In the same way, the guide we have provided you to confront your fears won't help unless you take the first step and apply what you learn to your daily life. Freedom awaits you on the other side of your fear, but you're going to have to take the first step.

Facing your fears is a lot like climbing a mountain. However, if you haven't noticed, mountains are a beast and not easily conquered. It's a process taken one step at a time as you carefully navigate rocky ground, obstacles, weather changes, and unforeseen challenges. Conquering the mountains of your fears takes commitment to staying the course.

A few years ago, my friend Sierra and I decided to take a spontaneous trip up to Yosemite Valley to fulfill our dream of hiking Half Dome. We literally decided two days before we hit the road and let me just tell you, we were NOT prepared for what lay ahead. It was a 16-mile hike that took us 11 hours and left us gasping for air as we reached 8,839 ft elevation. When we reached the sub dome (the base just before the top of the mountain) we were only about thirty minutes from reaching the top, but after hours of climbing, this point in our journey proved to be the most difficult. As we stopped to take a short break, I turned the corner and was shocked to find a woman lying down in between two rocks with her shoes off and her hands over her face. I immediately ran over to make sure she was okay. Startled by my friend and me, she sat up and explained to us what had happened. Thank GOD she was alive, I don't know how I would explain to authorities after carrying a dead body off a mountain. "Officer, I swear, she was already dead when we found her! I know we ate all her snacks and stuff, but have you made that hike? It ain't easy!!" Gosh, that would be a nightmare! Thank God that wasn't the case. She was a middle-aged woman named Alexis and she had a panic attack while hiking with her husband. She was so afraid that something bad would happen to them and couldn't get passed her fear so she gave up and told her husband to go on without her. First off, if my man abandoned me on a mountaintop I'd have some words for him! But that's another topic for another time. I sat down next to Alexis and began to encourage her. She was so close to reaching the top...I couldn't let her give up that easily! My friend and I began to encourage her and share our own struggles in conquering this mountain. Light began to enter her eyes as she looked up considering our words. We invited her to hike with us and committed to patiently walk the rest of the journey alongside her. Alexis was so encouraged, she put her shoes back on and said, "Ok, let's do it!" I learned something so powerful in this moment: fear can't exist when love surrounds you. Alexis felt alone in her struggle and she settled into fear accepting it as her fate. Yet when my friend and I related to her pain and shared our struggle with her, our love lifted the anxiety that isolation offered and her fear appeared less rational. Somehow, our presence and words of hope gave Alexis the confidence to access courage she already possessed. Can you imagine how fearless we all would be if we offered more invitations to walk the journey with others and surround them with love?

When we approached the dome we still had 100 ft of steep climbing left with only cables to hold onto. This, by far, was the most dangerous part of the hike. I went ahead and positioned Alexis in the middle between me and Sierra and told her not to be afraid because we were with her. The climb was steep and scary. Every few steps I'd turn back and check on Alexis. "How are you feeling? Just take it one step at a time. There's no rush. You're doing great." About halfway up I asked Alexis if she felt ok with stopping and taking in the view. She said yes and we stopped to memorize the vantage of this breathtaking moment. Alexis gasped and had a wide smile on her face. She exclaimed with excitement. She wasn't afraid like she was before, even if her legs were a little shaky, she was conquering her fear and it was paying off! As we reached the top of Half Dome, I got to record Alexis surprising her husband as she fulfilled her dream and showed fear who's boss! Sierra made it up just behind us like a champ (she was carrying a thirty-pound backpack with all our beef jerky and precious snack items) and we embraced taking in the moment, feeling thankful to have reached our destination and celebrating the freedom of a new friend.

[Sierra, Alexis and I on top of Half Dome in Yosemite]

Alexis was totally fearless and all it took was one step. There is a verse in the bible that says, *"This is my command--be strong and courageous! Do not be afraid or discouraged. For the Lord your God is with you wherever you go."* (Joshua 1:9, NIV). What this verse tells me is that there's a difference between *feeling* afraid and *being* afraid. Being afraid causes you to allow the feeling of fear to hinder you from reaching your full potential. It depletes you of strength and robs you of your purpose. However, feeling afraid is a natural part of life and doesn't have to end in a negative experience. Fear creates resistance and resistance is sometimes the very thing we need to dig deep and become who we were created to be. Just because you feel afraid doesn't mean you have to let it consume you and take up residence in your thoughts. Sometimes feeling afraid is a sign that you are approaching danger-- in fact, that is exactly what your brain is triggered by that creates a sense of anxiety. Fear is an alarm that goes off in your brain telling you not to do something that could be potentially harmful. Given the right scenarios, this is a good alarm to listen to. The feeling of fear tells us not to get too close to the edge of a high rise building. This is a healthy feeling we should listen to in order to preserve our lives. However, this feeling becomes unhealthy when it is triggered by trauma, wrong beliefs or irrational thoughts that are rooted in deep wounds. We want to encourage you to begin to make note of when this alarm is going off in your life and resulting in unhealthy patterns of anxiety and chaos. When the feeling of fear comes you have a choice to either give up and hide away in your fears or allow God's presence to give you the strength to break free from the overpowering emotions and rewire your fear alarm system, making it healthy again.

Watching Alexis overcome her fear and achieve her dream gave my moment on Half Dome priceless value! It gave it purpose beyond accomplishing my personal goal, which ultimately made it more enjoyable. Are you, like Alexis, allowing fear to rob you of the willpower to take the first step towards a difficult decision? Maybe it's fear of what other people think, fear of failing, fear of being rejected, fear of missing out or fear of commitment. These are all very real feelings, but they don't have to consume you and keep you trapped. God has gone before you, just like I went before Alexis and walked the journey *with* her. God is shouting back to you, "Baby, I'm with you. You can do this. Don't be afraid!" In the same way, Alexis was able to conquer her mountain of fear, believe you too can dig deep to access a courage that is already within you. The illustration below serves as a guide to help paint a picture and give you practical strategies that will lead you through your own journey of confronting your fears to find real freedom:

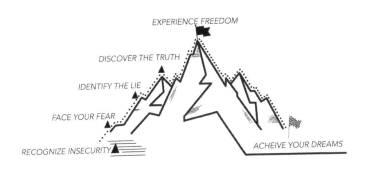

**Base Camp 1: Recognize your insecurities.** Insecurity is the first sign that fear is eating away at your dream. Insecurity causes you to feel inadequate and incapable of greatness and it overcompensates to impress others. Pride is at the root of insecurity, and fear is at the root of pride. Admitting your insecurity and locating the areas of your weakness is step one.

**Base Camp 2: Face your fear.** Our initial reaction when we encounter fear is to run from it. But we must face our fears head-on in order to overcome them. Position yourself to engage with your fear without hesitation. Do the daring thing: make the call, submit the application, have the hard conversation, sign up for the race, or whatever it might be. TAKE ACTION to face that fear.

**Base Camp 3: Identify the lie.** Many fears are built out of the lies we have believed about ourselves. We build false realities out of these lies and anticipate negative outcomes. Lies deceive you to believe that you will never find freedom from your past or present torment. These lies try to convince you to give up and settle for a "good enough" life. You can learn to recognize these lies by discerning the voice that condemns you. Lies always tear you down, but you can choose to reject them and replace them with the voice of truth.

**Base Camp 4: Discover the truth.** There is a voice of truth that is always speaking to you. It is our responsibility to tune our ear to recognize this voice and follow it. Having faith leads to knowing truth. Eventually, the lies that we have believed will fade away and the truth will outlive any deceptions. The voice of truth always speaks encouragement. It inspires positive imaginations and doesn't entertain fantasies that build a false reality. The truth is, YOU were created for a purpose and there is a uniqueness about you unlike anyone. But you must discover this for yourself in order for it to become your reality.

**Peak of the Mountain 5: Experience freedom.** Freedom is found in total surrender as you reach the top of your mountain. You are free from the struggle, you have faithfully stayed the course and overcome your fears. You can rest, breath, and take in the sights. You have won the battle. But your mountain top experience is not just for you. Freedom is fully enjoyed when shared. With your mountain of fear now beneath you, it is now time to lend freedom to those still living in fear, hiding out between the rocks of their torment. Your journey is not over yet.

**Completion of Journey 6: Achieve your dream.** Now that you have overcome your fear and conquered your mountain, it is time for you to dig deep into your purpose and achieve your dreams. You must journey onward and move into new territory of possessing the promises of God. Your purpose comes alive in new beginnings as you do the hard work of diligence to bring your dream to pass. Now is not the time to settle or give up. It's time to enter into your destiny and achieve your dreams with your fears now behind you.

These six steps are designed as a guide to help you navigate your personal journey of facing your fears. I dare you to stick with this book and apply these principles to your life and see the results of becoming unhindered by fear in all you pursue. Maybe you thought you could never do a particular thing. This book will empower you to have faith in yourself. Maybe you thought you could never identify with a faith-based belief or have a relationship with Jesus. This book will help you see past the stigmas placed on Christianity and teach you how to have faith in God (fast forward to page 192 to read a story of one of our friends who walked through this journey). God's love is written for you on every mountain. He faithfully pursues your heart and attention with every wave. Nothing scares Him about your past or even the mistakes you will make in your future. Everything in creation is designed to captivate your heart and invite you into the adventure of faith. You might be surprised by how exhilarating and freeing it actually is to allow yourself to have faith-- or if you already have a solid faith foundation, perhaps you've questioned how to go deeper into discovering your purpose and identity that is immovable by what others say about you. This book will empower you to overcome every big or little fear you may have and give you practical guidance to living a life unhindered. Doctors may have prescribed you several medications to help you cope with your anxiety. We believe there is a path to freedom that can be attained by prescribing truth. Treat each section of this book like you would your medications. Take them in doses, like a shot of courage injected into your veins, invigorating you with new hope to believe the best is truly ahead. Apply the daily challenges and share what you've learned with your friends on social media. In addition to this book, we have made the online E-course available for FREE on our website (Fearlessco.org). That's right, Oprah moment happening right here!! YOU GET AN E-COURSE, YOU GET AN E-COURSE, YEAHHHH!!! Always wanted to do that! We want you to be fully equipped and empowered to take on this life and be ready for whatever it may throw at you.

May you courageously pioneer through unknown terrain, overcome the obstacles of doubt, and thirst for a continual quest to lay hold of your purpose. May you become fearless as your mountains find their place in the rearview mirror of your life. And may you get the literal Fear out of your head and start LIVING!

**You've got this!**

# FEAR OF TAKING RISKS

One of my favorite things to do in the world is go surfing. I'm telling you it's the greatest feeling out there! Yet amongst all the fun, there are times where the waves test me way beyond my limits. Surfing has truly taught me how to be a true risk-taker. The risks are endless and there's no guarantee you won't get bruised, stabbed in the eye with the nose of your board (yeah, that happens), or held under by a wave for far too long. Did I mention, my favorite risk of all: a chance encounter with a great white shark! You might be wondering why I still continue to surf when the risks are so high. I get it, it's crazy! But would you believe these risky moments are the reason why us surfers love it so much! Not only is it incredibly fun, but it gives us an opportunity to taste a fearless moment. As a wave rolls in, it's as if the ocean is saying to me, *"I dare you to be fearless."* In that moment I

25

have two options. I can either allow fear to paralyze me and let the waves roll by, or I can accept the challenge and paddle into it! The first option is within my comfort zone and I hear a little voice inside my head telling me to play it safe. The second option pushes me outside of my comfort zone, entering into uncharted waters and potentially rewarding me with the most exhilarating experience. There is no guarantee I am going to make it into the wave without wiping out. Even if I do all of the right things, there's a chance something could go wrong.

It's important to remember in life that you will never arrive at a place where there is no risk. It's a risk to get out of bed, it's a risk to get in your car (especially if you drive in Miami! SHEESH!), it's a risk to show up to work; nothing is guaranteed. You may be surprised as you weigh out your decisions how some options that appear safe are actually quite risky.

So what's the antidote to risk-itis? How do you shut down that voice that tells you to play it safe? I found comfort from King David, one of the most heroic dudes in the Bible. He says, *"In God I have put my trust; I will not be afraid. What can man do to me."* Sounds to me like David had enough of fear holding him back and made the decision to swing all the way in the direction of God. By putting his trust in God and deciding to not hide away in fear, a supernatural confidence came to him. Trust in God + choosing to not be afraid = confidence to be fearless. The confidence we are looking for will only come when we step out to DO it. Trust in God as he makes you fearless to achieve your dreams. I promise the reward is worth the risk.

# Get the [F]ear out of Your Head

Today's challenge:

1. Get into a quiet space and close your eyes. Visualize yourself in the midst of your fear. Instead of imagining the worst outcome, imagine yourself succeeding.
2. Write down the reward of the risk you are struggling with and put it in front of you daily.
3. Do other things outside of your comfort zone like hiking to a high elevation, singing in front of a crowd, dancing in public, or spending time serving others in need. **God will use every step of faith you take and any step taken in faith is a step in the right direction.**

# FEAR OF MISSING OUT

Is it just me, or does scrolling through Instagram sometimes make you nauseous, too? I'm telling you, if I had a dollar for every post that made me feel like a total loser I'd have enough money to pay for a couple therapy sessions to help me get over my social media addiction, ha! Now, of course, I'm kidding, however, it can sometimes feel that extreme when my focus is set on wishing I had someone else's life, instead of realizing everything I do have. As I see my friends posting epic pictures of their travels and fun times that I didn't get invited to, immediately my life feels insignificant and I begin to envy their adventures. I can remember these two friends I actually introduced to each other one time and they totally hit it off. I felt excited to have made such a beautiful connection for them, even considered going into the friend matchmaking business (potential Shark Tank idea?). But then I started seeing them posting all of these epic adventures of them going snowboarding, surfing and drinking handcrafted coffee WITHOUT ME!! I jokingly commented TFTI...which is code for Thanks For The Invite. They would comment back "lol" and I thought, surely they just forgot to give me a call and next time they will invite me. Well, you guessed it. Next thing I know they are in Australia together, living their best hipster lives and here I am sitting on my couch at home feeling resentful that I ever introduced them. I mean, shouldn't I be entitled, at the very least, to a pity invite for introducing them? It took me a while to get over it and not be bummed every time they hung out without me. By the way, if anyone ever messages you TFTI, you have my full permission to tell them to get it together!

The fear of missing out is real, but it is perpetuated in this digital age more than ever. Social media can be a powerful tool used to encourage others or a weapon used to tear others down. We can allow what we see coming from everyone's highlight reel to inspire us or dig into our insecurities. Let's be honest about the social world of Instagram: as cool as it is to stay connected to our friends, it isn't an accurate depiction of day to day life. The real-life moments, like changing your cat's litter box, aren't exactly Instagram worthy and before you know it, you are trailing down a road of comparison.

I think we can all agree that life is more enjoyable when we are satisfied with what we have and who we are. The fear of missing out can cause us to lose touch with our significance. FOMO is not only a crappy feeling, but it robs us of the joy of seizing the moment and celebrating others. The Bible says, *"So be content with who you are, and don't put on airs. God's strong hand is on you; he'll promote you at the right time,"* (1Peter 5:6 MSG).

FOMO can literally create anxiety for you out of thin air. But it doesn't have to. You have the power to CHOOSE what you will focus on.

## Get the [F]ear out of Your Head

Today's challenge:

1. Choose to direct your thoughts towards what you have instead of what you wish you had.
2. Go through your Instagram account and unfollow accounts that don't encourage positive emotions in you. Steer away from the explore page as much as possible so you don't get sucked into the black hole of despair.
3. Save some adventures for yourself by not posting them to social media.
4. When you see a cool adventure posted by your friend, call them and ask them how it went. Celebrate your friends and be inspired by their wins!

EMPOWER EMPOWER

" Define who you are in the shadows and don't be afraid to bring that worth into the light. "

GREG BURGESS

FEARLESS CO.

fearless.co_ • Following

fearless.co_ The lonely seasons have the potential to develop you & refine your vision for your future. Nothing is wasted.

5w

estessss 🔥 🔥 🔥

5w   Reply

brandialxndra Love this!!

5w   1 like   Reply

— View replies (1)

Liked by estessss and 109 others

OCTOBER 24

Add a comment...   Post

32

# FEAR OF REJECTION

Rejection is one of those things in life that just makes you cringe at the idea of it. It's painful, hard to navigate and just down right a blow to your ego. I recently experienced rejection in a relationship that ended abruptly. One day this person was telling me everything a girl wants to hear: "You're my dream girl. I never imagined I'd find someone like you." All the heart eyes. Four days later, the script flips and now I'm hearing things like, "It's complicated. I'm confused. You just came out of nowhere." To get to the bottom line, homeboy was trying to tell me he had met someone else and was more interested in her than me. I was so afraid of being rejected and deeply wanted him to choose me. Yet, how could I sit around and wait for him to figure out his feelings? Would it be me or this mystery girl? How did I end up on The Bachelor? Would I make it to the final rose ceremony? My mind was swirling and all I knew was that I was worth more than this. I was terrified, but chose to end things with him and move on, even though it meant having to walk through rejection.

That wasn't a fun experience and one I would never like to repeat. But it taught me that sometimes rejection is the doorway to something greater. Regardless if things end the way you hoped or not, closure is found in rejection. However, where we get hung up is when we don't close the door all the way and we allow resentment, bitterness and fear to hold us hostage to the past. We will relive our rejection over and over if we never forgive and move on into the new things God wants to do in our lives.

Rejection may not feel good at first, but fearing it holds us back from making pivotal decisions that could lead us into our ultimate desire. Sure, things didn't end like I'd hoped with that guy, but that rejection re-directed me into God's plan and will ultimately lead me to the person who will see my value.

There may be times when you will be rejected, but God will say, "Go back and try again." Don't give up on the first try. If it's God's plan, even the greatest impossibility can't hinder you from finding success. Let the rejection roll off your shoulders and give you the confidence to get back up and keep fighting.

# Get the [F]ear out of Your Head

Today's challenge:

1. Make a list of 10 things you like about yourself. Repeat them out loud and look at them daily. Confidence is key to shaping your self-worth and building the courage to take a risk at being rejected.
2. Map out a plan for how you want to approach your challenge. Come up with a backup plan if it fails and invite a friend in on your process so they can support you.
3. **JUST DO IT! You got this.**

# FEAR OF BEING VULNERABLE

The word 'vulnerable' has had it's go around amongst my community over the last couple of years. Yet, it's become one of those things I've completely lost touch with. The Merriam Webster definition of the word 'vulnerable' is *"capable of being physically or emotionally wounded."* This doesn't sound like a warm invitation to a life of freedom. Wounding? Ouch. Yet, vulnerability is exactly what is required for us to live free from fear and honest before God, ourselves and others. C.S Lewis nails it in this quote from his book, The Four Loves:

*"To love at all is to be vulnerable. Love anything and your heart will be wrung and possibly broken. If you want to make sure of keeping it intact you must give it to no one, not even an animal. Wrap it carefully 'round with hobbies and*

*little luxuries; avoid all entanglements. Lock it up safe in the casket or coffin of your selfishness.* **But in that casket, safe, dark, motionless, airless, it will change.** *It will not be broken; it will become unbreakable, impenetrable, irredeemable.* **To love is to be vulnerable.**" *(The Four Loves, p. 169)*

Shame, doubt, and insecurity create a breeding ground for fear. Once we allow fear to claim real estate of our mind, vulnerability becomes our enemy. Instead of partnering with truth to find freedom, we partner with the lies our fear tells us and mistake fear as our protector. *"No one loves you. Don't listen to them, they don't know your story. You'll never make it so why even try. Everyone always ignores you. Just act like it doesn't bother you."* This is the soundtrack of fear that echoes in our head. Vulnerability encourages us to allow others into our insecurities to help us, but this is always at the risk of getting hurt.

I can't think of a person who was more vulnerable in history than Jesus. Jesus poured his life out for people who hated him, daily choosing to love his enemies and serve them. At the end of his earthly life, Jesus lived out the definition of vulnerability, making his body open to being physically and emotionally wounded. Yet, the pain he would suffer was a result of our sins and what we deserved, not him. Jesus' vulnerability paid the price for our freedom. He stretched out his arms on the cross in the greatest act of love and didn't try to hide how painful it was. Yet, because he knew you and me were on the other side of his resurrection, he chose to lay down his life for you and me. I don't know about you, but hearing this gives me the courage to be vulnerable in my own life.

Instead of putting on a filter and pretending like everything is perfect, I want to live like Jesus and offer my vulnerable self to those who least deserve it, even if it's painful. I want to give my all and not hold back out of fear of how others may perceive me or criticize me. I think you want to do the same too.

## Get the [F]ear out of Your Head

Today's challenge:

1. What things make you feel the most vulnerable? Opening up about your feelings? Reaching out to make a new friend? Telling someone you have feelings for them? Admitting that you are wrong?
2. Write down what makes you feel the most vulnerable right now in your life. Ask yourself what you have to lose in a worst-case scenario. Now ask yourself, if what makes you feel vulnerable is worth losing what's at stake?
3. Write out a prayer and ask Jesus to help you make a courageous, vulnerable decision, just like he did. He will show you the way.

# FEAR OF
# THE UNKNOWN

While we were filming our online course in Yosemite National Park, we came to a sign along our trail that said, "Caution: Rock Fall. Enter at Own Risk." The sun had gone down, it was pitch black and the temperature was starting to drop. My friend Ebie turned to me and said, "Esther, this is not a good sign." I looked ahead at the path. There was a waterfall we would have to run through and who knows what other roadblocks lay ahead. Though the path was uncertain, I had hiked it enough times to know how to navigate the terrain even if there were unforeseen challenges. I turned to Ebie and said, "It's ok, I know where the path leads!" We gathered our group together and ran through the freezing cold waterfall that led us into knee-deep water. Our flashlights revealed snowy mounds, fallen trees, and massive rocks that blocked our way. Ebie began recording a voice memo of her final goodbye's and Will to her husband and children, in her dramatic fashion. Things were only starting to get crazy. As the flashlights illuminated our path we could only see what was revealed one step at a time, noises echoed in the distance and the chance encounter of a California black bear haunted our minds. After a few more hours of hiking, we made it off the trail by 10 pm that night. After it was all said and done, of course, our favorite part of the adventure was that moment we faced our uncertainty and decided to traverse through all of the elements leading us to our victory.

This story serves as an illustration for our lives. When faced with an uncertain situation we have the option to recoil in fear or view the unknowns as an invitation to be courageous. God tells us in the Bible, *"I will instruct you and teach you in the way you should go..."* (Psalm 32:8 NIV). Just like Ebie had to trust me to guide the group down the path, we need to trust God to instruct us in our daily lives. We need to believe He has already gone before us and knows where the path will lead.

Maybe you are facing some unknowns in your own life. Perhaps it is uncertainty about what school you will get into? Or if your test results will come back positive? You may not know what's to come, but don't allow a caution sign hanging in front of your unknown to deter you from pushing through to your victory. **The wild unknown favors the brave- the adventurous ones who take the roads less traveled.**

# Get the [F]ear out of Your Head

Today's challenge:

1. Practice filtering your thoughts as your mind wanders. What are some of those noises in your life that are haunting your mind?
2. Get into the Bible and find a verse that speaks to you about your specific situation.
3. Paste that Bible verse everywhere in your house and put it in your calendar to remind you daily to not worry.
4. Release the need to be in control and find certainty in God as you trust Him to guide you.

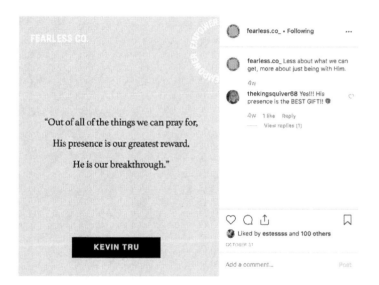

FEARLESS CO.

"Out of all of the things we can pray for,

His presence is our greatest reward.

He is our breakthrough."

**KEVIN TRU**

fearless.co_ • Following          ...

fearless.co_ Less about what we can
get, more about just being with Him.

4w

thekingsquiver68 Yes!!! His
presence is the BEST GIFT!! 🎁

4w  1 like  Reply
— View replies (1)

♡  ◯  ⬆                          🔖

Liked by estessss and 100 others

OCTOBER 31

Add a comment…                    Post

# FEAR OF BEING MISUNDERSTOOD

When I was eleven, I got to sit next to my crush in the back of a pick-up truck with all my friends as we drove around a park late at night. I'll never forget that night because we all played a game of telephone and I got to whisper in my crush's ear! But what made this moment even more unforgettable wasn't just my crush sitting next to me, or even the ridiculous game of telephone that was going on— it was one of my guy friends, who also happened to have a crush on me, sitting on the other side next to me. We were all sharing a blanket, and at one point of the night, me and my friend put our heads under the blanket to play with a flashlight or something weird homeschool kids did back then. I don't know, but the point is everyone started their own game of telephone about us, and before we knew it, rumors spread like wildfire! It was one giant misunderstanding. Everyone was convinced we had kissed, and it took weeks to clear up.

Sometimes, misunderstandings happen because we

miscommunicate. Other times they happen because others perceive us the wrong way. We aren't responsible for how other people will react, but we are responsible for what we say and do.

There are definitely things we can do to avoid misunderstandings. Staying away from the appearance of evil is one of them. Not putting my head under a blanket with a boy would have been the wise decision in that situation, but hey, you live and you learn.

We often find ourselves in places in life that challenge our ability at communicating. The connection between our heart, words, and actions can sometimes lose touch, and we fall short of communicating our true intentions in those situations. This shouldn't cause us to draw back or feel discouraged to communicate. It should challenge us to get better and learn how to refine our actions or our words in order to allow our hearts to be fully seen and heard.

Maybe you posted something on Instagram you thought was funny but ended up offending a lot of people (been there, done that). Or perhaps you said something to a friend that you thought would be helpful, but instead, it made them feel insecure and self-conscious. Whatever your situation may be, know it is in your power to change the narrative and adjust your approach to reconnect your heart with your actions. Misunderstandings will happen in life, but we can always do a better job of ensuring our intentions are transparent and visible for others to see.

# Get the [F]ear out of Your Head

Today's challenge:

1. Have you felt misunderstood by a friend, family member, or your community? First, quit the broken record in your head that is repeating back your failures. YOU ARE NOT A FAILURE. You are a good friend,a good sister/brother, and a good leader.
2. Maybe it wasn't your fault, or maybe it was. Regardless, it's important to remember that humility will get you further in life and being right. Take time to reflect on your words and actions and evaluate what you could have done better.
3. Ask those who were involved in the misunderstanding to meet with you privately. Explain your pure intentions and ask for their forgiveness.
4. You aren't going to win them all, and that's ok. Not everyone wants to understand you. Just walk in love and keep moving forward.

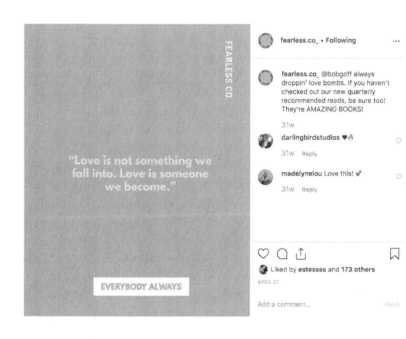

fearless.co_ • Following

fearless.co_ @bobgoff always droppin' love bombs. If you haven't checked out our new quarterly recommended reads, be sure too! They're AMAZING BOOKS!

31w

darlingbirdstudios ♥️🍃

31w  Reply

madelynelou Love this! 💕

31w  Reply

Liked by **estessss** and **173 others**

APRIL 27

Add a comment...                    Post

# FEAR OF HEARTBREAK

Heartbreak comes in many different forms: a break-up, losing a loved one, missing old friendships, or leaving your home to move somewhere new. Whatever the heartbreak is, there is often a temptation to build a wall around your heart. There is a line from a song called 'Hello My Old Heart', by The Oh Hellos that really struck me when I heard it:

*'Hello, my old heart*
*How have you been?*
*How is it being locked away?*
*Don't you worry, in there, you're safe*
*And it's true, you'll never beat*
*But you'll never break.'*

I performed this song with a friend at a coffee shop one time. My friend was so nervous, he literally threw up before we performed and then we had to share a mic. Poor guy! But that verse of the song got me thinking about how often we try to self-protect and think we're doing ourselves a favor when really, we're robbing ourselves of a chance at being loved.

I experienced my first heartbreak in a relationship a few years ago. I was in L-O-V-E with a surfer dude that had dreadlocks down to his waist and every other word he used was "gnarly" or "rad." It was pretty much love at first sight for both of us. Our relationship was great for a while, but eventually, our vast differences came to the surface and I knew I had to end it. When the relationship failed, my heart hurt like never before. Some days it felt like a 50-pound weight was sitting on my chest. It became difficult for me to trust others out of fear that I would get hurt again, so I built a wall around my heart and didn't want to let anyone in. Instead of having healthy conversations about it with my friends, family, or even the guy I broke up with, I turned to busyness to try to distract me from the pain. I was so deeply hurt, but the grief of heartache was too much to bear, so I did my best to cover it up like it had never happened. Needless to say, that didn't last long. I finally came to the realization that I needed God to restore my heart and give me hope again. I forced myself to have a healthy conversation with the guy. Then I spontaneously bought a ticket to Australia to attend a conference with a few of my friends. I met some incredible guys at this conference who truly taught me how godly guys should treat women. One guy, in particular, made me feel so special, and I realized I had dramatically lost sight of my value and what I deserved.

My walls began to come down, my heart began to heal, and my hope was beginning to be restored again.

Through that experience, I was met with the reality of this verse, *"The Lord is near to the brokenhearted."* (Psalm 34:18 ESV). Navigating heartbreak isn't an overnight process. It can sometimes take months or even years to fully regain wholeness. But this time isn't wasted if you are intentional about seeking out the One who is your Healer and not allowing distractions to keep you enslaved to old habits.

## Get the [F]ear out of Your Head

Today's challenge:

1. Are you afraid of letting someone close or committing to a new relationship? Talk to someone who gives godly wisdom about your attachment to that heartbreak. Healthy conversations lead to a healthy heart.
2. Make a decision today that you aren't going to stay broken. Don't allow past heartbreaks to steal your dream and hold you prisoner to your past.
3. Remember, the waiting is never wasted.

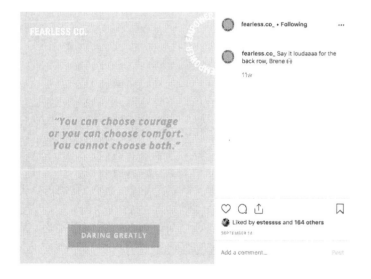

# FEAR OF
# LETTING PEOPLE DOWN

Are you the peacekeeper in your family or friend group? I'm kind of like that in my family, a diplomat of sorts, or the nucleus chip holding all the cheese and toppings together on a plate of nachos. I'm the one that clears the air, settles conflict, and visits all the siblings to ensure we are keeping the peace. Though I love keeping us all together, I tend to lose myself in the mix and care more about what my family thinks about my life decisions, rather than pursuing my own peace and doing what's right for me. I have struggled with the fear of letting my family down for years but recently have been able to find freedom.

A few months ago, I accepted a job with my brother's company that seemed like my dream job at the onset. I believe in my brother so much, he could literally ask me to sell birdseed in a chicken costume, and I'd do it. As the weeks passed at the job, I began to feel uncertain about my decision. Yet, I was determined to push through and shrugged my feelings away, assuming they were a result of starting a new job. Instead of pulling back to re-evaluate, I committed even more and was determined to make it work. I was so afraid of letting my brother down I was undervaluing myself. As I was praying about it, I woke up one morning, realizing I've been trying to force myself into this role because of my fear of disappointing my brother. I've been unhappy, sad, and lacking vision for my future because I've been striving and stressing to please others and have not been true to myself.

There comes a time when we have a choice to make: forfeit your peace to please others or choose what's right for you at the expense of letting someone down. The voice of shame will try to convince you that letting people down will turn you into a let down. But that isn't true. You are not a failure for trying something, giving it your best shot and discovering it's not for you. You are not a let down; you are a brave one.

It takes courage to say yes to a big decision and give it the time and attention in your life to see if it's the right commitment. And it takes just as much courage to gracefully decline the opportunity, knowing full well that someone else is a better fit than you.

Don't allow the fear of letting people down keep you stuck in a place in life that you know deep down inside is robbing you of peace. Are you staying in a certain location because you are afraid that moving away from your family would break their hearts? Are you forcing yourself to show up to a job every day that you hate because you are afraid it will let your spouse down? Whatever it is that is holding you back and keeping you stuck; it's not worth your peace and joy. YOU are valuable and your feelings are valid. Perhaps your discontentment doesn't need to result in a relocation or leaving your job, but it should cause you to pause and pray about what God is speaking to your heart through the unsettlement.

One of my favorite verses is found in Psalm 37:23-24, *"The Lord makes firm the steps of the one who delights in him; though he may stumble, he will not fall, for the Lord upholds him with his hand," (NIV).* This verse reminds me that as long as I delight in the Lord, He will guide me. Even if I stumble, He's got my back, and He's got yours too.

## Get the [F]ear out of Your Head

Today's challenge:

1. Who are you afraid of letting down? Maybe it's your parents, your friends, or even yourself. Ask yourself, do they love you because of what you do, or just because of you?
2. Have a conversation with the person you are afraid of letting down (or yourself). Ask them to go on the journey with you to find a solution and give it time to resolve.

# FEAR OF NOT BEING GOOD ENOUGH

Measuring up can often seem unattainable when we're surrounded by a world of comparison. When I was a teenager, I teetered on the edge of an eating disorder as I hated my appearance and couldn't see my true worth. I was constantly chasing perfection and trying to achieve this elusive idea of what I thought I should look like based on what I saw around me. I was clothed in insecurity and living in constant shame.

It's become increasingly easier to compare ourselves to others in the digital age we live in. But the reality is, when we measure ourselves against others, we will always lose. No matter what kind of car you drive, it's never cool enough. No matter how much money you have, someone else always has more. No matter how famous you are, the attention is never enough.

Well, I have good news for you: you will NEVER be good enough. Really, though, that is good news! NOTHING in this life will ever be ENOUGH to measure your worth. You were made with eternal value, and only your Maker, God, can affirm your worth.

The fear of not being good enough comes from a place of shame. Deep down, we believe we are too much or not enough and look to others as if they have what we need. This mindset will always leave us feeling empty. Matthew 11:28 says, *"Come to me, all who labor and are heavy laden, and I will give you rest"* (ESV). The fear of never being good enough is an endless cycle. God offers you rest and total confidence that you are perfect just the way you are.

Do you battle with thoughts of being inferior around people who appear more talented or attractive? Do you work tirelessly and strive to be the best, but never seem to measure up? Perhaps your efforts seem like they are lacking because you have lost sight of your true worth and are living in a shame-driven mindset. **Earthly measurements could never equate your true value. Only an eternal measurement created by God could accurately define your worth.**

# Get the [F]ear out of Your Head

Today's challenge:

1.  Quit the negative talk! Don't use sarcasm to mask your insecurities. Watch what you say about yourself and only speak positive affirmations.
2.  **Take a break from social media or unfollow accounts that don't make you feel encouraged.** One rule I stick to is never clicking the explore page, as it always seems to discourage me and distract me from my purpose.
3.  Make a list of 10 things you like about yourself. Recite this list out-loud in front of the mirror and ask God to help you see yourself the way He sees you.

# FEAR OF GETTING HURT

On a surf trip to Mexico, I got separated from my friends while surfing in some big waves one day. All of a sudden, a huge set of waves appeared out of nowhere! I began to paddle as hard as I could, but it was too late. The monster wave came crashing down, taking me down with it. I tumbled underwater for the greatest ocean beating of my life, only to resurface and get pounded again by another giant wave! Thankfully, I fought through and made it out of the ocean that day with just a few bruises and a renewed respect for the ocean.

After that experience, it was harder for me to surf the rest of the trip. Each time I paddled out, my previous wipe out replayed in my mind like a broken record. I held back for fear the same thing would happen again. I was so afraid of getting hurt or held under again and lost trust in my ability to be a strong surfer.

I wasn't too proud of myself for allowing fear to ruin a great trip and refused to allow that incident to rob me of my passion forever. After that experience, I had to rebuild my confidence while surfing. I overcame my fear of getting hurt by putting myself in situations where I could expand my courage. I upped my game in surf training, practiced breath holds under water, and at the gym. I was determined not to allow fearful memories from the past to dictate my future. There is a healthy fear that helps us to avoid danger, but when the fear of getting hurt hinders you from enjoying your life, it becomes a stronghold.

The fear of getting hurt is a result of a lack of trust, which then turns us into control freaks. Either we don't trust other people, ourselves, or we don't trust God. Sometimes, we are the ones who cause the hurt by the choices we made. Sometimes other people hurt us and it's not our fault. **Although we are not promised a pain-free life, God can be trusted to guide us through painful times.** Don't allow the memories of your past to hold you captive to fear in an attempt to control your future.

# Get the [F]ear out of Your Head

Today's challenge:

1. What is causing you to be afraid of getting hurt? Is it issues within family relationships? Stop bracing yourself for the worst! Stop replaying the past. Realize that the opportunity in front of you is a chance to start over.
2. TRUST God! He is ultimately in control, even though you think you should be.
3. Make a list of the things that have hurt you in your past. Evaluate how those painful situations have wounded you and ask God to heal you of that pain.

# FEAR OF BECOMING DISCONTENT

No one wants to live an average life. No one wakes up in the morning and says, "Man, I'm just feeling the pressing desire to be average today." People don't do that. We are all born with a desire to achieve greatness and feel fulfilled in our work, personal lives, and relationships. We want to find contentment and resolution in the things we aspire towards. Even if we don't tap into that potential within us, it's there calling for us to step into it.

That's why I believe so many people, especially us Millennials, struggle with this fear of becoming discontent with their lives. We don't recognize it as a fear because we are driven by ambition to keep striving towards our goals.

But deep down inside, we are afraid that if we were to slow down, stop and catch our breath, we would be discontent with our lives.

Have you ever felt this way? Afraid of being alone with yourself? Do you feel a sense of pride and self-worth connected to your job title, achievements or even ministry? We often can get into this rhythm of constant busyness. So much so, that we lose touch with true rest and intimacy with Jesus. Or maybe you've never felt that before and you battle that restless feeling. Whichever category you fall into, I get it, I've been there and it ain't fun.

Recently, I've been challenged to slow my roll. God literally dared me to cash in the life I loved and held dear in Southern California and trust Him on an adventure of transitioning into being a full-time writer and speaker. My greatest fear in taking that risk is that I wouldn't return back to California, would have to settle in a place that is uninspiring and lose my passion for pursuing my dreams. The fact that I had this fear at all was enough to make me do it anyway!

On my drive across the country to South Florida, I realized how boundless God is. His plans are so beyond the limitations and confinements we've imagined. I believe we make ourselves suffer due to the wrong mentality, telling ourselves God is asking us to sacrifice what we love and settle for something less amazing because He wants us to prove our love for Him. But that is so twisted. Jesus says in Matthew 7:19-11, *"Which of you, if your son asks for bread, will give him a stone? Or if he asks for a fish, will give him a snake? If you, then, though you are evil, know how to give good gifts to your children, how much more will your Father in heaven give good gifts to those who ask him!"* God is not trying to take anything from you; He is 100% trying to multiply what is already in your hands by helping you get a loose grip on what you are currently clinging to.

During my season here in South Florida, God has done wonders in my heart, relationships, and personal life.

I have learned what it means to truly allow God to fulfill the desires of my heart in His way that far exceeds my limited capacity. He has given me the freedom to dream so much bigger than I could have had I stayed attached to what I previously had. He has also given me permission to go and do what He has placed in my heart. God is on our team! He wants to see your dreams realized more than you do!

Don't allow the fear of being discontent to stop you from exiting your comfort zone to explore what God may have for you somewhere else. Perhaps it's not a permanent shift, as in my case, but allowing your heart to be open to it gives God the freedom He needs to move in your life.

# Get the [F]ear out of Your Head

Today's challenge:

1.  Does letting go of what you have scare you? Maybe it's a job switch, commitment to a relationship, or relocation. Write down what those fears are and ask God to give you the courage to face them.
2.  DO IT. **Confidence comes in the doing.** Remember, God is with you and wants to multiply what's in your hand.

# FEAR OF CHANGE

Summer is my all-time favorite season. As I'm writing this, California is transitioning from summer into fall. I'm always sad to see summer go. If I could, I'd wear a bathing suit, shorts and flip flops year round! Yet, no matter how long I fight it, the seasons *will* change.

For some, change is invigorating. For others, change is stressful and feels like the entire world is crumbling. Whichever category you fall into, one thing is certain- change is *unavoidable*. Life is full of changing seasons that challenge our ability to adapt and grow.

When I was 21, I moved from Miami, Florida, to Huntington Beach, California, nearly 3,000 miles away from home! This was a HUGE change, and I spent the next five years learning how to navigate this season of independence. It was hard, painful, and I went through a period of grieving the life I had left behind.

I can remember standing in line for security after saying a tearful goodbye to my family on the day that I moved. I became so fearful of the change about to take place and uncertain if I was really doing the right thing. With tears streaming down my face, I handed my ticket to the security agent. As I began to walk away, he stopped me and said, "I know right now it's really hard and for a time it's going to hurt, but God wants you to know you're going to be ok. You're going to be so happy." At that moment, it felt as though God reached down from heaven and gave me the biggest hug.

Looking back on that now, after seven years, I am amazed at how good God has been to me. It was incredibly hard at first, but every challenge helped me grow and develop my character to be who I am today. Though the transition was painful, God gave me a new home and a new life in exchange, and I truly am so happy.

Change hurts, and it is difficult, but if we embrace it and move forward, we will grow into our full potential and enjoy the life God has handpicked for us. God encourages us that, "There is a time for everything, and a season for every activity under the heavens" (Ecclesiastes 3:1, NIV).

**We fear change because we can't imagine loving something any more than we do. But God already knows your future.** He knows all of the things in your life you have yet to experience and what will bring you joy, beyond where you currently are.

If you are afraid of a new season approaching or uncertain about a decision that would change your life drastically, take a deep breath, and be assured that it's going to end well. Whether it's your current opportunity or another down the road, God will give you the confidence to walk boldly into the next season.

## Get the [F]ear out of Your Head

Today's challenge:

1.  Is God inviting you to make a change in your life, but you are too afraid to let go of what you have? Write down an area of your life you know needs a boost.
2.  Talk with God about the decision you're facing, trust Him with the outcome, and don't let the fear of change hold you back from starting something that could be beautiful.
3.  Call a good friend and discuss the internal conflict going on inside of you that is challenging that decision. Allow them to encourage you and hold you accountable to make the right decision.

FEARLESS CO.

YOU HAD A PURPOSE
BEFORE ANYONE
HAD AN OPINION.

EDIE HEPWORTH

fearless.co_ · Following          ···

40w

macdenno YES 🤚
39w   Reply

nightsofunity 🤙 🚀 🤙 Come on!!!
39w   Reply

erinmpruett So good!!!!
39w   Reply

wgm9320 @deb.paniagua
39w   1 like   Reply

h3h_hali I needed this today

♡ ◯ ↑                              🔖

Liked by **caitlinzick** and **458 others**
FEBRUARY 26

Add a comment...                   Post

# FEAR OF
# WHAT OTHER
# PEOPLE THINK

'A Walk To Remember' is one of my all-time favorite movies. I believe guys secretly love this movie too but dare not admit it for fear of losing their man card. There's this scene at the beginning of the movie when the two main characters, Landon and Jamie, are sitting next to each other on the school bus. Landon turns to Jamie, a conservative Christian girl who was known to wear a sweater with every outfit, and says, "You don't care what people think about you?" Jamie looks him straight in the eyes, smirks, and simply says, "No." And puts her headphones back on and turns up the volume. Oooh, smooth, very smooth! I remember watching that scene for the first time and wishing I could be more like that. Yet, the reality was I cared more about what other people thought of me than what I thought of myself. It affected everything I did. How I dressed, talked, ate, and acted around my friends. I often said no to doing things outside of my comfort zone because I was too afraid of people looking at me, even though deep down inside, I wanted to do those things. I was so self-conscious and it was eating me up inside. This self-consciousness was rooted in a lack of confidence in myself.

The fear of what other people think is also translated in the Bible as the fear of man. In Proverbs 29:25 it says, *"The fear of man lays a snare, but whoever trusts in the Lord is safe"* When we fear others, we give them the place of God in our lives and allow their thoughts, actions or words to dictate how we feel about ourselves or even confuse the actual voice of God in our lives. This fear can get us into a lot of trouble if we allow it to fester in our hearts.

I finally hit a turning point when I graduated high school and moved to Daytona, Florida, for a summer to work at a Christian Camp. Being in this new environment provided space for me to confront my fears head-on as they began to surface. At this point, my fears had consumed me and were holding me captive to an eating disorder and an unhealthy desire for constant affirmation from others. One day, the leaders of the camp gathered us together. At the end of the night, they called up anyone who was feeling sick. I had a cold, so I went up with a few others for prayer. My whole team circled around me and began to pray. I thought I had just gone forward to receive prayer for my stuffy nose, but God had other plans. At that moment, I felt God touch my heart. I can remember feeling the presence of God surround me. I felt Him exchange my insecurity with a seed of confidence and set me free from the fear of man. I knew that stronghold on my life was gone. From that day on, I never struggled with an eating disorder again. In fact, right after the meeting, I was so hungry, I treated everyone to McDonald's, which I would never have eaten in a million years at that time!

As I allowed God to transform the way I thought about myself, I became less concerned about what other people thought about me. In fact, this sense of freedom has exploded in my life, and I almost never consider what other people think of me and am able to be my authentic self no matter who's watching. I've learned to focus more on being true to who God has made me to be. I'd rather give people something worth thinking about and inspire them with my life than worry about if they do or don't like me. Psalm 8:4 says, *"What is mankind that you are mindful of them, human beings that you care for them?" (NIV)* This verse is a reminder that God in heaven is thinking about you. He cares for you and has given you a place in His family to live in total freedom. At the end of the day, it is all about pleasing God, not others.

## Get the [F]ear out of Your Head

Today's challenge:

1. Do you struggle with feelings of self-consciousness around others? Take time to consider the moments you feel most aware of this and make a mental note of the environments that make you most uncomfortable.
2. Examine your thoughts about yourself. Do you have low self-esteem, or are you overly critical about yourself, constantly trying to 'improve' your appearance or yourself?
3. Seek counsel from a mentor or older friend who can offer wisdom for your specific situation. Be open and transparent with them, and ask them to pray with you to take authority over this stronghold on your life and find freedom from the fear of what other people think.

*fearlessly*
*fearlessly*
*fearlessly*

fearless.co_ • Following

fearless.co_ Here's how you cor
Monday.

44w

meta.for 🔥 🔥

44w   Reply

theredwoodhouse 🦅

44w   Reply

mixxyogastudio 🙌 💜

44w   1 like   Reply

mixxyogastudio I love what you
organization is about :)

♡ ◯ ⬆

Liked by estessss and 146 others

JANUARY 28

# FEAR OF TRYING SOMETHING NEW

I'm the kind of person who fully embraces anything new. New clothes, new foods, new experiences, new cars, new friends-- all the new, I'll take it! New things just have a special feeling to them, like a sense of wonder to explore the mystery of the unknown. It's always exciting to have new things in our lives, yet, there are some things in life that I genuinely love more because they are old, broken in, and comfortable. Certain areas of my life are just good as is, no need to upgrade. But sometimes God wants us to think beyond what we've known and step into the new with an open mind.

In Isaiah 43:19, it says, "*See, I am doing a new thing! Now it springs up;* **do you not perceive it?** *I am making a way in the wilderness and streams in the wasteland*" (NIV). One of the key takeaways in this verse is the question God asks: do you not perceive it? In my opinion, when God asks a question, it's not because He doesn't know the answer, but He is trying to get you to catch on to what He's doing. You see, **we will never find what we're not looking for.** If we don't have the eyes of faith to perceive what God is doing, and just keep looking for the old pattern and the way we are familiar with, we won't be able to see the new thing God is doing.

Often times, these new things occur in a season of feeling empty, void of purpose, or lost for direction. In this verse, God uses the imagery of a wilderness and a wasteland to describe the kind of landscape He is building on. What the heck? Doesn't God realize prime real estate is obviously in a luscious coastal area with lots of beauty surrounding it? I mean, If I'm going to build a new house, you're not going to find me walking through Death Valley scoping it out. Wildernesses are dry, hot, and a place where things are known to die, not thrive. Wastelands are...well, wastelands! They are a place where you go to dump all your junk and never look back. Yet God took the two most desolate concepts and used them to paint a picture for you. Even in a season or a place where you feel like you are dying, God sees a prime location for something beautiful to be built. Even in a place of total shame and resentment of the time you have wasted, God sees a perfect opportunity for a fountain of life to come gushing forth out of your pain. What you see as an end, God sees as a new beginning. But the question is, will you perceive it now?

God never takes an old thing and refurbishes it. He always starts with nothing and turns it into a masterpiece. Are you willing to let God start from scratch in your life and remove the old things that are broken? Even the old things that you love; that are comfortable and broken in? Are you willing to part with that old habit, mindset, relationship, or position you are in to embrace the new God has for you?

## Get the [F]ear out of Your Head

Today's challenge:

1.  What are some old things in your life you could do away with so God can make room for the new? Write down what first comes to mind.
2.  Think back on another season of your life that may have seemed hopeless and remember how God came through for you then. Spend time imagining how God will move on your behalf again in this new season.
3.  **Thank God for all He has already done and ask Him to give you the eyes to see the new thing He has for you.**

ONE OF THE GREATEST WEAPONS THE ENEMY USES IS ISOLATION: CAUSING YOU TO FEEL LIKE YOU ARE ALL ALONE AND NO ONE UNDER-STANDS YOU.

*Don't believe the lie.*

YES YOUR PATH AND PURPOSE ARE UNIQUE, BUT THERE ARE ALWAYS PEOPLE BESIDE YOU TO WALK WITH YOU.

AMPLIFY AMPLIFY

LISA MARACINE. FEARLESS CO.

fearless.co_ • Following

fearless.co_ Don't believe the lie. Power packed nuggets ft. @lisamaracine from yesterday's podcast on singleness + dating

7w

lisamaracine Yes!! We're here for each other

7w  1 like  Reply

madelinegjohnson whew

7w  1 like  Reply
—— View replies (1)

jkbarth

7w  1 like  Reply

Liked by estessss and 227 others

OCTOBER 10

Add a comment...          Post

# FEAR OF BEING LOVED

As crazy as it sounds, many people often live in fear of receiving the very thing they want. Being loved can make us feel vulnerable and exposed. Sometimes we don't believe our unfiltered self is truly worth loving. We may react to the love people offer us by working really hard to put on our best performance so we feel deserving of it, or we push them away and retreat into our fear.

If we dig deep, we might find that our sense of value is less connected to who we are and more connected to what we do. I found this to be true in my own life recently as I was evaluating a friendship that I have with a close friend and her family. I couldn't help but notice how anxious I would get around them and the way I over-extended myself to prove to them how thankful I was for their friendship. Not only in this relationship, but in many other cases, I have forced my greatest efforts to impress others simply because I haven't felt deserving of their love. It was as if there was an invisible scale that I felt was weighing my worth, and I was doing everything possible to measure up.

My greatest fear in receiving their love was that they wouldn't truly love me for me if I wasn't doing something that benefited them. This kind of mindset tormented me for years and trickled into many of my relationships. Recently I read a verse in 1John 4:18 in the Passion Translation that totally wrecked me, *"Love never brings fear, for fear is always related to punishment. But love's perfection drives the fear of punishment far from our hearts.* ***Whoever walks constantly afraid of punishment has not reached love's perfection."*** This verse shook me as I realized no matter how much I preach about love, I won't know the first thing about it if I don't know how to receive it.

The devil wants to torment you by manipulating you to earn someone's love and telling you that is normal. Without even realizing it, you begin to devalue yourself by adopting a mindset of striving and rewards based relationship. This mindset tells you If you do good, you will be loved. But if you do bad, you will be rejected. This is a religious mindset that is all based on your works, not on the value of who you are.

Jesus came to restore your value. It was the price He paid for you on the cross that gives your life eternal worth-- worthy of a man dying for you, so you can live a free and beautiful life. Sometimes we know this by default, but not by revelation. When our value becomes a reality to us, we are able to find freedom from a posture of shame and receive the love and grace God and people have to offer us.

# Get the [F]ear out of Your Head

Today's challenge:

1. Sometimes our fear of being loved can surface in different behaviors. Do you get extremely physical in romantic relationships? Do you have a broken relationship with someone in your family and are afraid of letting them close? **Have a conversation with God about this and ask Him to reveal to you the ways you haven't been able to receive love.**

2. Choose one person in your life that you have a difficult time feeling worthy of their love. Write them a letter completely unfiltered of how you feel. Include in the letter a solution to improve the relationship and ask them to forgive you for keeping them at a distance. Mail the letter or plan a time to meet with them in person. You are worth loving, believe it!

FEARLESS.CO

AT SOME POINT, WE
BECOME SO ATTACHED TO
OUR NONSTOP, BUSY
LIFESTYLE THAT IT
BECOMES A SAFE PLACE.

LIBERTY FLEMING

---

fearless.co_ • Following         •••

fearless.co_ Liberty is sharing some
serious truth over on our blog about
staying true to your restful moments in
the midst of day to day busyness. It is
fearless to take a moment to breathe
and know the world isn't dependent on
you. | LINK IN BIO

38w

ally.m.smith 🐚 SHOOOOOOT

38w   3 likes   Reply

thekingsquiver68 So true! Busy
seems to be a status symbol these
days

38w   3 likes   Reply

♡  ◯  ⬆                          ◻

🌐 Liked by estessss and 226 others

MARCH 12

Add a comment...                  Post

# FEAR OF NOT HAVING ENOUGH

Two years ago, I decided to go back to college to finish the degree I had started in my early 20's. This decision required me to pull back on my hours at work so I could focus on studying. Yet, cutting back on my hours meant I wasn't able to make as much money. I can remember those first few months of school and stressing so much about paying my bills. It was a constant worry and caused me to isolate myself from my community and use any spare time I had to babysit or work overtime in order to reach my budget for the month. This insane schedule wasn't sustainable, and I found myself getting extremely burnt out soon after. In prayer one day, I felt the Lord lead me to Proverbs 3:5-6, *"Trust in the Lord with all your heart and lean not on your own understanding; in all your ways submit to him, and he will make your paths straight,"* (NIV). It's a verse most Christians know well, and to be honest, I didn't know what this verse had to do with money or helping me pay my bills.

But I could sense God directing me to the word *trust*. In order to trust God with my finances, I needed to do something outside of the realm of my understanding. I said I was trusting God, but my actions proved that I was completely reliant upon myself.

I made the decision to quit striving and stressing and start trusting God with my finances. **If he had called me into that season, I knew He would provide.** I committed only to babysit a certain amount of hours and not over-analyze my budget to ensure I would make enough to pay my bills. I determined to take each day as it came and build my faith by focusing on what God had already done, knowing He would provide for my needs.

As each week passed, I remember looking ahead at the due dates of my bills approaching and saying, "Wow, God, can't wait to see how you pull this off!" Though I was somewhat nervous about how this would pan out, I was ready to see God move. During this time, I was continuously blown away as God showed up time after time, meeting my needs in such beautiful ways. In fact, things started getting so crazy! I began to make a list of all the financial miracles that happened in my life in that season. Here are just a few: Found a check in my wallet for $210 (apparently I lost it 6 months prior), $50 for winning a turkey gobble contest, $250 from Uber that showed up in my bank account randomly after an error in their system, various donations made to Fearless Co., $600 check in the mail from IRS (almost threw it away 'cause I thought it was fake!), $400 flight voucher I used to fly home to visit my family, AND THE LIST GOES ON! To this day, I am still adding to this list and praising God for all of the financial miracles that He provides both through job opportunities, ministry, and fun special surprises like the ones I listed.

I am so thankful I took the step of faith to trust God and not carry the burden of not having enough. It was easy, and sure it was a bit of a creative season. Some weeks I ate cheese quesadillas for every meal (no shame). At one point, I didn't go grocery shopping for three months, yet I always had something to eat, even if it was a slightly creative meal. Though that was a stretching season, I wouldn't take it back for the world because it built my faith and taught me how to truly trust God as my Father to take care of me.

## Get the [F]ear out of Your Head

Today's challenge:

1. Does financial burden stress you out and cause you to strive to make ends meet? Are you living pay-check to pay-check and becoming stingy with your money? Take time to evaluate your spending. Are you generous with your friends, family, and church?
2. Ask God to guide you in taking steps of faith to surrender your worries and give Him full access to your trust.
3. Commit to making a change. Whether that be educating yourself about finances, looking for a better job, or doing what I did. Determine what that change is and DO IT!

FEARLESS CO.

It's not our
responsibility
to be a perfect
human, but
it is our
responsibility
to speak truth
to others.

JEN BARTH

fearless.co_ • Following                    ...

fearless.co_ In case you never listened
to the Podcast episode 'Victim to
Victory' by our girl @jkbarth , stop
what you're doing and go listen! It's
POWER!

33w

♡ ◯ ⬆                                    ⬚

Liked by **estessss** and **156 others**

APRIL 9

Add a comment...                        Post

# FEAR OF FAILURE

Bodybuilders use the phrase "lifting to failure" to describe the process of lifting until you can't lift anymore-where muscles have been pushed to their limit, causing them to tear and grow bigger. Despite the pain, failure has the potential to make you the strongest you have ever been.

Naturally, we often connect failure with a negative experience. Failing has the potential to make us feel embarrassed and ashamed, and when we make a mistake, we automatically identify ourselves as being a failure. With this mindset, it's easy to believe our worth is connected to our aptitude to perform. Robert F. Kennedy once said, *"Only those who dare to fail greatly can ever achieve greatly."* The fear of failure limits our ability to dare greatly and has caused many people to self-sabotage their dreams. This is often the result of identifying *as* a failure. But, failing doesn't have to define who you are, rather it has the power to refine you and make you better. If we allow failure to shame us, we lose confidence, stop trying, and eventually give up. But failure is a natural component in the process of achieving our dreams.

In fact, Thomas Edison made 1,000 attempts at achieving his dream of inventing the light bulb. To onlookers, he appeared to be a constant failure at his craft, yet he never saw it from that perspective. Instead, Edison saw every failed attempt as a solution to the problem. In his response to a reporter who remarked about his failures, he replied, "*I didn't fail 1,000 times. The light bulb was an invention with 1,000 steps.*" According to Thomas Edison, every attempt that ended in failure was a step closer to the solution. This mindset is empowering!

**We must be vulnerable to the experience of failure and see it as a catalyst to fulfill our dreams.** The truth is, failure gives us the opportunity to respond to life's challenges with a positive outlook and see beyond our present circumstances. Recognizing our areas of weakness is actually an advantage because it helps us discover what needs to be adjusted in order to reach our goal. With this perspective, our failures will begin to build our weaknesses and turn them into strengths.

Letting go of past failures and confronting current ones will empower you to be stronger. Don't be overcome by failure and live in fear. Instead, allow your failures to build your weaknesses into strengths. Know that God will guide you to make the best decisions even when you fail. God is with you, picking you up and showing you the way. Be courageous and develop a resilience for failure as you become stronger in the pursuit of your dreams!

# Get the [F]ear out of Your Head

Today's challenge:

1. Are you afraid of moving forward with an idea, dream, or conversation because you're afraid it won't go as planned? Write down the past failures that have held you back or the failures you are afraid of making, and next to them write "I AM NOT A FAILURE" in big, bold letters.
2. Are you feeling discouraged and like you've hit a dead-end in life? Maybe you've reached a certain age and feel you aren't where you thought you'd be by now, and it is making you feel inferior. Take time to evaluate these thoughts about yourself.
3. Define a healthier definition of failure by redefining what success is. Write out your definitions and go back to them often to remind yourself you are one step closer.

A PRAYER FOR WALKING THROUGH GRIEF

"ALIGN MY EXPECTATIONS, MY HOPES & MY BELIEFS WITH WHAT YOU WANT TO DO IN THIS MOMENT.

*SIT WITH ME IN THIS PAIN.*

SIT WITH ME AS I ADJUST MY EXPECTATIONS.

GOD, I WANT TO HOPE WITH YOU IN THIS."

FEARLESS CO.

EBIE HEPWORTH

AMPLIFY AMPLIFY

**fearless.co_** • Following

**fearless.co_** May this prayer be a weapon of courage to lift you out of despair & onto a horizon of hope. ☀ "Even when bad things happen to the good & godly ones, the Lord will save them & not let them be defeated by what they face." - Psalm 34:19 TPT

9w

**thekingsquiver68** Love this!

9w   1 like   Reply
    View replies (1)

**linimae** That's so good!

9w   1 like   Reply
    View replies (1)

Liked by **estessss** and **137 others**

SEPTEMBER 26

Add a comment...                    Post

# FEAR OF
# MOVING ON

I have a little picture frame on my desk that says, "Begin again, Darling." I got it at a women's conference at my church one year, and it has always served as an inspiration to me in numerous seasons where my journey at a certain place came to an end. Moving on isn't easy, especially when you aren't ready to do so.

It can be scary to move on after a break-up, loss of friendship, or significant life change. We fear that what is ahead will be a disappointment compared to what we have left behind. We fear that if we hope again, we will get hurt again. Moving on to the uncertain future is difficult, but it is necessary to fulfill our dreams.

When I first started surfing, I learned a valuable lesson about moving on. Waves would rapidly approach, and as I would begin to paddle, I would continue to look back at the wave, afraid that it would crash on me. This resulted in me getting taken out by the wave, and it happened over and over again. Frustrated, I talked to a friend about my experience, and she told me I needed to look ahead in the direction I wanted to go in order to properly catch the wave.

The next time I paddled out, I followed her instructions and immediately made improvements! Her guidance not only made me a better surfer, but provided a great illustration for life. If you constantly focus on what's behind you, it will distract you from the opportunity that is presently in front of you. God tells us to, "Forget the former things; do not dwell on the past" (Isaiah 43:18, NIV). You are wasting energy worrying about the past when God wants to do something brand new. You will never even be able to see what lies ahead in the future if you keep looking back to your past.

Letting go of the past is the first step to moving on. Is there a situation in your past that you haven't confronted? Addressing these issues is necessary in order to find freedom.

It's time to begin again. This means making the decision to stop dwelling on the past and recognize your habits that are hindering you from moving on. Have you been talking about your break-up too much? Maybe you've been reminiscing a little too much of the 'Good ole Days.' It's time to pull your thoughts out of yesterday and anchor your hope in the joy that's to come.

**You will find love again. You will get another opportunity. You will have more 'Good ole Days.'** It's time to look forward, anticipate a new and exciting adventure, and allow yourself to ride the wave of opportunity. It's time to turn the page and start writing a new chapter as you enter into the adventure of moving on!

# Get the [F]ear out of Your Head

Today's challenge:

1. Take time to journal about the memories that are holding you in a state of grief. Write down the areas that need to be addressed and the people connected to the situation. Pray that God would give you the courage to confront your past and let go.

2. Perhaps you need to forgive someone or even forgive yourself. Consider reaching out to a friend or mentor who knows you well and ask them to walk you through the emotions you are feeling. Godly counsel will always guide you to a place of freedom.

FEARLESS CO

Gratitude combats pride, which we often find is the root of being burned out.

EBIE HEPWORTH

fearless.co_ • Following ...

fearless.co_ This is the absolute truth! ✨ This week's episode unpacks the first three months of launching Fearless Co. and how burnout managed to sneak up on us. Have you ever found yourself burnt out and if so, how did you overcome it?

33w

anjelmurphy Yessss and I love ...

33w  Reply

prime_proper so good!!!

33w  Reply

kymberfaith Dangggg so good!!!

♡ ◯ ⬆                        🔖

Liked by estessss and 139 others

APRIL 11

Add a comment...                Post

# FEAR OF
# BEING STUCK

When I asked my friend the other day what his greatest fear was, he shared with me that the idea of settling down and being stuck terrified him. In fact, it was such a paralyzing fear it was hindering him from entertaining a serious relationship with anyone. Though he desperately wanted to find someone to share his life with, he found himself self-protecting and pushing people away because he was afraid of being stuck in a boring life.

I can understand his pain and think this is a common fear for many people. Whether we fear being stuck at a 9-5 job, the concept of committing to one person forever, or stuck in one place too long-- this fear has become an epidemic amongst millennials. Though we think we are doing ourselves a favor by keeping a safe distance from the things we fear will make us stuck, oftentimes we are actually doing a disservice to our dreams and hopeful futures. Instead of freedom, we are actually keeping ourselves in a prison of restrictions thinking we're living the good life.

I began to share with my friend that he could actually find exactly what he's looking for if he shifted his perspective about feeling stuck in these commitments. In one sense, it can be healthy to be cautious about situations that would make us feel stuck. It's good to be in touch with what energizes you and what kind of future you want. **We should never be so comfortable that we don't embrace change or dream into what could be. However, there is a steadiness that commitment offers that is an adventure and unraveling of wonder.**

Often times, the fear of being stuck comes out of a place of wanting to control everything in our lives. You could be the most free-spirited person and want to just live in your van and travel the world, having no plan or agenda, yet deep down, you are desperately trying to control your life by disconnecting from a conventional lifestyle. I find nothing wrong with the desire to live the nomad life. However, I believe being driven by fear in any area of our life is an unhealthy place to be. Psalms 37:5-6 says, *"Commit your way to the Lord; trust in him and he will do this: He will make your righteous reward shine like the dawn, your vindication like the noonday sun,"* (NIV). The word 'way' in this verse really stands out to me. We have our own way of doing things that are not always God's way. If we don't live surrendered to His way, we will end up going in a completely different direction. But when we commit our way to Him, His ways start to become woven into our heart and our hopes and dreams begin to build around His eternal perspective of our lives. We are promised that if we give God access to how we live, He can be trusted to outshine anything we could do on our own. God wants to do great things in our life *with* us, not just for us.

When we commit our way to God, we can be confident

He will never abandon you or cause you to be stuck anywhere. When you have an eternal perspective of your life, things become less black and white and more colorful in the understanding that this life is a partnership with God. Trust that anyone He puts in your life is there to multiply your sense of freedom, not take it away. There's no such thing as being stuck when you're living the adventure of faith.

## Get the [F]ear out of Your Head

Today's challenge:

1. Have you been dancing on the line of commitment or passive in thepursuit of your dreams because you fear being stuck? Write down the one area of your life you feel most afraid will keep you held back.
2. Maybe you already feel stuck in the season you're in and don't know how to shake that feeling. Close your eyes and begin imagining the most impossible ways you could find joy in this season. Imagine crazy things like winning a million dollars or you getting your dream job.
3. Make a list of three things you think are impossible in this season or about the thing you fear. Write out a prayer and thank God for doing the impossible in your life and vow to commit your way to Him today.

_"God is going to reveal me as a flawed human being as fast as he can and he's going to enjoy it, because it will force me to grapple with real intimacy."_

·Scary Close

**FEARLESS CO.**

fearless.co_ • Following

fearless.co_ Don't walk, RUN to get Scary Close by Donald Miller. It will CHANGE EVERYTHING.

12w

gracewhilewewait 🔥 🔥 🔥

12W    1 like    Reply

⸻ View replies (1)

joneal1205 🔥 🔥 🔥 🔥 🔥 🔥 🔥 🔥 🔥 🔥

12W    1 like    Reply

⸻ View replies (1)

Liked by estessss and 167 others

SEPTEMBER 6

Add a comment...                                   Post

# FEAR
# OF DYING

As a little girl, I would often be afraid of my parents dying or even fearful that I would suddenly die. I'm not sure what planted that thought in my innocent mind, but it was so real to me. My parents traveled quite a bit for missions when I was a child, and I can remember being so restless every night before they were meant to fly out, crying to my mom because I was afraid their plane would go down. It was a tormenting image in my mind that gripped my imagination and wouldn't relent. The fear was so intense, that even on normal fun days I was unable to have fun with my friends and instead spent the day concerned that something bad would happen to my mom and dad.

I can remember one day while I was having one of these sad moments, I began to explain to my mom through my tears that I was mad at God because He would have to take my parents away from me one day. The idea of heaven scared me and didn't make sense to be separated from the people I loved. My mom tried to explain to me that heaven is actually a wonderful thing and that one day I would be reunited with them again. Although that seemed like a comforting thought, it still terrified me to imagine the grief of loss and the unfathomable concept of heaven.

Death is such a wild thing to comprehend. There are times when people we love die prematurely, and we cannot understand why. Even when death has its place at the end of a long-lived life, it still feels like we're being robbed. This is because death was never God's original plan. Instead, God planned for us to live in a constant heaven on earth experience in relationship with Him. Death was introduced as a result of sin and placed on the lifespan of humans as a limitation to short-circuit the time we have to engage in sin and evil. When Jesus entered the equation of humanity and redeemed our relationship with God, He also defied death and gave us a new perspective of dying that is now an open door to eternal life. As a Christian, death isn't the end; it's the first day of truly living in the unshielded presence of God.

I found great courage in 2 Corinthians 5:6-8, *"That's why we're always full of courage. Even while we're at home in the body, we're homesick to be with the Master— for we live by faith, not by what we see with our eyes. We live with a joyful confidence, yet at the same time, **we take delight in the thought of leaving our bodies behind to be at home with the Lord"*** (The Passion Translation). There is a perspective shift that happens when we embrace an outlook of faith rather than what our carnal eyes can see. Recognizing that our bodies are a temporary living space for our spirit will set us free from the hopeless feeling death brings.

Jesus refers to death as sleep, and in many cases in the New Testament, Jesus actually brought people back to life. There are times in our life when people die from sickness or freak accidents that we know for certain was not God's plan for them as these instances defy God's character as a loving Father. This is a big conversation to have, but in light of overcoming the fear of death, we can find comfort and courage in a perspective shift. **Perhaps we need to have a greater revelation of heaven and what it means to truly live than focus on how to not be afraid of dying.**

## Get the [F]ear out of Your Head

Today's challenge:

1. Is the fear of death (either of yourself dying or your loved ones) keeping you from living life to the fullest? Are you afraid of moving away from your family for fear of what may happen while you are away? Or perhaps you're afraid of flying or taking risks because the feeling is so real. Take time to determine what this fear is rooted in.
2. Read 2 Corinthians 5:6-8 every day for a week. After you read it, close your eyes and begin to imagine the scenarios that scare you most. Ask Jesus to go with you into those moments and show you how to shift your perspective. Change how the story ends by imagining a really happy ending. Practice this daily and anchor your hope in eternal life.

# FEAR OF DISAPPOINTMENT

Disappointment downright sucks! But the only thing worse than being disappointed is being wired for it. Before we even get a chance to be let down, fear creeps in and tries to convince us that it's not going to end favorably. The voice of fear invades our thoughts with endless chatter filled with doubt. Before we even see evidence of our desires not being met, we begin to lose hope as we anticipate the worst.

I experienced the fear of disappointment when I applied to go back to school a few years ago. It had been five years since I last studied, and although I was excited, I was also really afraid I would be disappointed by taking this risk. Thoughts plagued my mind for months leading up to school. 'What if I made the wrong decision? What if I'm meant to do something else?' Worry crept in as every waking thought was consumed by doubt. One day, I was on the phone with my school advisor at the college I was applying for. She was answering any questions I had about the school, and in the middle of the conversation, I stopped and said to her, "Cat, I'm honestly just so scared I'm making the wrong decision." She immediately responded with, "Esther, that is totally normal and a sign that you are taking a leap of faith. You're in the sweet spot of grace. God won't disappoint you." That phrase, 'the sweet spot of grace' stuck with me for months. It's like this terrifying place of not being in control and yet totally trusting that God will meet you where you are, even if it doesn't end how you hoped. This brought so much freedom to my life.

There is an empowering passage in Job 11:18 that we can find comfort in, *"Having hope will give you courage."* It doesn't say, "Lower your expectations and see how it turns out." Rather, it encourages us to get our hopes up! I found comfort and security in having hope, and new thoughts began to come into my mind, 'What if this is EXACTLY what God has planned for you? What if you will be the happiest you ever have been? What if this is the next step to help you achieve your dreams?' **Hope gives me the confidence to trust my decisions are good and that God will lead me.** I don't have to hold back from fully expressing what I desire. Hope gives me courage to trust the process and believe for good endings.

Sometimes it can be difficult not to grow weary in the waiting period. This is often when we fear disappointment the most. People will tell you not to get your hopes up, but I believe you should get your hopes up as high as they can go! Psalm 38:15 says, *"Because I have placed my hope in you, LORD, you will answer."* (ISV). When you put your hope in God, you can't be disappointed. The time of waiting is created for us to grow. It's time to rewire ourselves for hope and stop bracing ourselves for fear of being disappointed.

# Get the [F]ear out of Your Head

Today's challenge:

1. What are you hoping for today that you are afraid will end in disappointment? What are the "what-ifs" that torment your thoughts? Write down the negative "what-ifs" and next to them write down the positive "what-ifs."
2. **Put your hope in God, and don't allow the fear of disappointment cause you to forfeit your dreams.** Begin to speak out loud the thing you are hoping for and allow God to write the end of the story His way. Let go of your fear of being disappointed as well as your need to control the outcome. God will far exceed your expectations.

FEARLESS CO.

EMPOWER EMPOWER

"The most important thing that ever happens in prayer is letting ourselves be loved by God."

THE RELENTLESS TENDERNESS OF JESUS

fearless.co_ • Following
Boise, Idaho
...

fearless.co_ Are you reading our quarterly recommended reads with us? If so, let us know! We want to know what you think!

30w

groverst Loving Present over Perfect...it's helping me walk away from finding my worthiness in the busyness to receiving it at the feet of Jesus and letting him direct my day, redeeming the time by focusing on what matters!

30w   1 like   Reply
······ View replies (1)

riverhouseboise AMEN 🙏

Liked by ascendchurchmi and 135 others
MAY 6

Add a comment...                    Post

# FEAR OF ABANDONMENT

One of my best friends grew up never knowing her biological father. However, she did have an amazing step-dad who took her in as his own and loved her deeply. Because of the way her step-dad loved her, she never felt the need to search for her biological dad. But a few years ago she and I were talking, and I mentioned how curious I was for her to find him. She finally decided she wanted to meet him and started to do some digging.

After some long talks with her mom, a little investigation, and a paternity test, my friend found her dad living 39 miles away from her home. Are you kidding me?! After reaching out to him, she discovered he had no idea she existed or that he was her father. This felt like the realest Jerry Springer show ever, and I was flipping out! My friend was just about to get married, so this couldn't have come at a better time.

The day they met, they walked up to each other, embraced, and immediately started crying. As her biological father held his daughter, now 29 years old, in his arms, he began to tell her these words, "If I had known, I would have wanted you. If I had known, I would have been there." My eyes swell up with tears just thinking about how powerful a moment this was. My friend shared with me how in this moment, she felt something shift in her heart and a deep lie she had always believed broke off of her completely. Because she never knew the full story about her biological dad, she had felt she wasn't wanted. She felt abandoned, and because her dad abandoned her, others would too. This was a recurring theme in her life, especially in relationships with guys. Guys would come into her life and leave just as easily. Every time a guy walked out on her it fortified the lie even more. Though she had been working through overcoming this fear and had found freedom in Christ, the words of her biological father resonated within her heart and only echoed the words of her heavenly Father, *"I will never leave you or forsake you,"* (Deuteronomy 31:6, NIV).

Perhaps you've felt abandoned by a parent or someone else you should have been able to rely on. You may be looking for the same closure my friend went looking for and hoping you, too, will hear those words. The reality is, not every story will end this way. What I find comforting is knowing that **our healing is not found in how the story ends, but is found in receiving affirmation from our heavenly Father.**

The fear of abandonment can often come from a series of relationships that have hurt us, people who have forsaken us, and situations that have left us with no closure. I believe my friend already was secure in who she was and didn't question her value, which is why she was never curious to find her biological dad. Though there was more healing that happened for her when they did meet, I believe she would have found that same freedom another way regardless of how the story ended, because she knew her heavenly Father would not abandon her.

# Get the [F]ear out of Your Head

Today's challenge:

1.  Have you felt abandoned or rejected because of a failed relationship or maybe even a job situation? Do you often fear others leaving you or giving up on you? Maybe you fear your partner will cheat on you because you've been cheated on before. Make a list of things people do, or might do, that make you feel insecure. Make a second list of ways you react to them. How can you change your reaction to be one of confidence and not insecurity?
2.  Memorize Deuteronomy 31:6 and allow your heavenly Father to love you deeply. If there is someone in your life you need closure with, ask God to show you if and how you should proceed.

# FEAR OF COMMITMENT

My friend Sierra and I had just begun our ascent on one of the hardest trails in Yosemite Valley: Half Dome. Halfway up the mountain, I was ready to call it quits. It would take us 10 hours to complete the 17-mile trek and reach an elevation of 8,842 feet. The most hiking I had ever done was take a walk in a park. Let's just say, we were in for a rude awakening.

There were many times I stopped to catch my breath and thought to myself, 'This is good enough, let's head back. What's the point of getting to the top anyhow?' My thoughts continued to weigh my decision to press forward. As we continued up the trail, we did everything humanly possible to keep our mind off of the agonizing pain in our legs. We sang songs, ate beef jerky, played 21 questions, and yet time seemed to be moving slower than ever. I wanted to give up so bad but was determined to finish what I had set out to do for bragging rights. if anything. And I'm so glad I did! The view from the top was breathtakingly beautiful and one of the most life-changing experiences I've had to date.

I learned a valuable lesson on that hike to Half Dome: **you have to be committed to the journey, not just the destination.** The path you take to get to where you need to go might be boring at times, but it's essential to stay committed to the journey each step of the way. There are times where it's not going to be fun, and we may be in pain, but if we focus on these challenges, we will miss out on the moment that could be just as memorable as reaching the destination itself. In fact, a moment Sierra and I almost missed out on during our journey was an encounter with a bear! As we were making our descent from the mountain singing, "Teenage Dream" by Katy Perry at the top of our lungs, all of a sudden, we see a giant mama bear about 15 feet away. Yep, we were about to be lunch. Not really, but it was pretty epic! Had we been complaining and rushing through the journey, we would have missed this crazy experience that invigorated us along the way and reminded us why we love to get alone in the woods. You never know what could happen, what you may see or what wild adventures are waiting for you.

The same thing is true for life, but the fear of commitment is a common theme for many young people who are struggling to find their way. The concept of signing a contract, getting married, relocating, or even choosing to stay somewhere that you have a hard time loving, can make you feel, well...STUCK. Without realizing it, the fear of commitment can cause you to slip into an apathetic lifestyle as you opt-out of plans with friends because you got a better offer or back out of a commitment because it was more work than you realized. Let's be real. Our generation SUCKS at commitments.

I will fully take the blame for how I've contributed to a

fear of commitment within our culture as I have often been the one to cancel plans or ghost someone because I found a better opportunity. I know, that's terrible, but it's true, and you can probably relate more than you'd like to admit. Not all commitments are fun or easy. Some commitments are a process, but if we don't commit to the process, we will never realize our full potential or achieve our dreams.

When we fear commitment, we tend to run from the things that will challenge us to grow. Apathy causes you to settle for a temporarily fulfilling experience. There are sacrifices that come with commitments, but there is also great reward, and the rewards are lasting.

## Get the [F]ear out of Your Head

Today's challenge:

1.  Do you often tell people you will show up and change your mind at the last minute? Do you overcommit yourself? Start making changes in your life by sticking to your word and following through. Make a mental note every time you say 'yes' to someone and determine to follow through with it no matter the conflict.
2.  What scares you about big commitments? Make a list and reach out to a mentor who has made these commitments. Perhaps you are afraid of getting married but feel more comfortable with the idea of moving in with your partner. You may think this is a safe common ground, but the root of it is fear. Reach out to a friend to help guide you (or if you don't have a mentor, reach out to me! My email is in the back of this book)!

EMPOWER EMPOWER

" Brave doesn't always involve grand gestures, sometimes brave looks like staying when you want to leave, telling the truth when all you want to do is change the subject... sometimes brave looks like boring, and thats totally, absolutely, okay. "

- Present Over Perfect

**FEARLESS CO.**

---

**fearless.co_** • Following

**fearless.co_** Our team recently read through 'Present Over Perfect' by @sniequist and all we can say is RUN, DON'T WALK to get your copy. If we created a reading community, would you be interested in joining?

44w

**myjoytribe** Yesss
44w   1 like   Reply

**vevans44** Yes!!!!
44w   1 like   Reply

Liked by **estessss** and **357 others**

JANUARY 23

Add a comment...                    Post

# FEAR OF
# NOT FALLING IN LOVE

As a kid, I loved to watch Mary Kate and Ashley movies and always turned into a puddle at the end of every movie when the music faded as they slow danced with their crush. What can I say, it was my guilty pleasure. Yet, early on in adolescence, I began to be so afraid of never falling in love. What if I never got my cheesy slow dance moment?! Girls are crazy.

As ridiculous as it sounds, fear has a way of taking our emotions and making worst-case scenarios seem unbelievably real. As I continued to grow up, this fear of never falling in love haunted me and tormented my emotions. The lie was only fortified after every failed relationship.

I found myself blaming others for my fear and masked my pain with harsh sarcasm as I always claimed to be president of the Single For Life Club! But the root of the

117

problem was my lack of self-worth, not in the way others valued me. I finally found freedom in my early twenties when I began to confront my insecurities and realize my true worth. As I worked through these issues and confronted my fears, I was able to uncover the lies I believed about myself and replace them with the truth. Today, I am no longer afraid of not falling in love. I know I am worth loving and deserving of a marriage that makes Mary Kate and Ashley on screen romance jealous.

**You are so worth loving. Repeat that out loud with me: I AM SO WORTH LOVING.** Good job! God promises that our future is full of hope (Jeremiah 29:11). He wants you to get excited about the plans he has created you for. But if you truly want to fall in love in a healthy way, you have to first see yourself the way God sees you. There are many opportunities to fall in love with toxic people that often leads to unhealthy relationships. Take time to become whole and fully confident in who you are before you allow someone else to affirm your worth. If you're afraid of not falling in love, chances are you probably aren't ready to.

# Get the [F]ear out of Your Head

Today's challenge:

1.  Write down 5 lies you have believed about yourself, followed by 5 truths and scriptures to accompany these truths. Hang them on your bathroom mirror and read them out loud every day.
2.  Watch your mouth! Keep tabs on the things you say and be watchful of masking your pain with sarcasm. Ask Jesus to help you change what you say by healing the wounds in your heart. You can be free from the insecurity that has held you captive and believe that the perfect love story awaits you in your future.

# FEAR OF
# FEELING EMOTIONS

I have always been an in-touch-with-my-emotions kinda girl. On average, I cry a good healthy cry at least once a day. Listen, it's totally normal, trust me. But a few years ago, I went through a season where my emotions became too much for me to bear, and instead of going to someone who could help me navigate them, I learned how to shut them down and not feel at all. I was too afraid that if I allowed myself to feel these things that I would become overwhelmed with pain and have an emotional breakdown.

Well, needless to say, it's never a good idea to stuff your emotions away for a rainy day. The more I refused to deal with my emotions, the more they piled up in my heart and weighed down on me like a pile of bricks. I would wake up every day barely able to breathe, with tears streaming down my cheeks because I didn't want to have to show up at work to pretend everything was ok. I hated my job and had lost touch with my purpose.

I had never experienced depression before, but in this season, I could feel a dark cloud hovering over me each day. I would have panic attacks at work when my thoughts would race, my palms would get sweaty, and my whole body felt like a thousand degrees. I felt so alone and didn't know how to fix it. Although it was one of the most painful seasons I have walked through yet, I never failed to cling to God's Word, promises, and presence even when all hope appeared gone. Even in the midst of my darkest hour and my deepest fears, God met me and carried me through.

About six months into this season, I recall having a conversation with my brother about my life. We were both in town visiting family for Christmas and taking a walk on the beach when he turned to me and said, "Esther, you know you don't have to have it all figured outright? You're putting so much pressure on yourself. You don't have to have it all dialed in right now." Tears began to stream down my face as the emotions I had stuffed down began to explode to the surface. I was so afraid of making a wrong move, so afraid of letting people down, so afraid of everything! In this moment, I finally allowed the pressure to release and my heart to feel again.

On the day I returned home to California after that trip, I hit my knees in my apartment and rededicated myself to the call of God on my life. I didn't know all the details or how it would all work out but I was committed to making a change. I knew my emotions were telling me to quit my job and begin getting serious about my passion to write and speak. I started serving as a youth leader at my church and was determined to show up even if I didn't feel like going. Little by little, God put people in my life that would help me find my way and lock into my calling again. Four months later, I launched an internship at Fearless Co. that was a springboard into the next season for our organization. God did so much in such a short amount of time, delivered me from depression and anxiety, and gave me a safe place in His presence to process my emotions.

Feeling challenging emotions isn't bad; in fact, they are often good indicators of pain in our hearts that have gone overlooked. **When you give yourself permission to feel your emotions in the presence of God and seek His Word to help you navigate what you feel, you will be empowered to use your emotions for His glory and your benefit.**

## Get the [F]ear out of Your Head

Today's challenge:

1. Have you been wrestling with anxiety or depression? Journal about the things you have been feeling and be real with yourself. Give yourself permission to not have everything figured out.
2. Make a notecard with Psalm 42:5 on it and read it every day: "Why, my soul, are you downcast? Why so disturbed within me? Put your hope in God, for I will yet praise him, my Savior and my God."
3. Ask Jesus to show you the steps to take to re-awaken your heart to your purpose and experience a healthy emotional life. Seek professional counsel or reach out to a friend to help you walk the journey.

EMPOWER EMPOWER

"TRANSITION WILL ALWAYS BE UNHEALTHY IF YOU DON'T KNOW YOUR TRUE IDENTITY."

ANJEL MURPHY

F — C

fearless.co_ • Following

fearless.co_ @anjelmurphy droppin' bombs on the latest podcast episode titled, "Trimming the Fat" □
11w

macenzie ✔️ @paisleybeach
11w   1 like   Reply

riverhouseglobal Come on!
11w   1 like   Reply
—— View replies (1)

elyzabeth_faith @jessemichael86
11w   Reply

Liked by estessss and 174 others
SEPTEMBER 12

Add a comment...                    Post

# FEAR OF SETTLING DOWN

My friend called me the other day to announce she was headed to the Canary Islands for a surf trip for 3 months. Yet another friend who was trading in her 9-5 job to live a vagabond life! I desperately tried to go on the trip with her, but the responsibilities of life kept me at bay. All I wanted to do was buy a Volkswagen van, travel up the coast, surf, and eat tacos! Is that really too much to ask?!

My friend's travel lifestyle was no surprise. Many millennials embrace gypsy living, backpacking, and wandering from place to place. The idea of settling down causes most young twenty-somethings to gag and go running for the hills. The thought of getting a real job, getting married, buying a house, and starting a family is scary! For some people, these are the dreams that energize their hard work. But for a lot of people, especially young adventure seekers, settling down feels like trading in their freedom for a boring life.

It's common to feel bewildered at the thought of making such major life decisions, but the fear of settling down is an indicator of immaturity. Adventure and travel have their place of purpose in our lives, but sometimes choosing to stay, grow roots, and build a sustainable life is the greatest adventure. The reality is this: fulfilling your dreams takes time, hard work, and commitment. Until we arise to the responsibilities that our aspirations require, our dreams will stay out of reach. Sometimes that means slowing down, focusing on what's most important, and prioritizing certain goals that align with creating our best future. Settling down doesn't mean you have to give up your sense of adventure, but rather it's a shift of mindset that is focused more on building legacy.

Maybe you're not ready to get married, buy a house or start making babies, but maybe the fear of settling down is causing you to run from the adventure you really crave: a stable future. It's time to take action and break free from wrong mindsets that are attached to this immature outlook. **Don't believe the lie that you aren't ready. You will never be more ready than this moment**.

There is nothing wrong with wanting to travel, and I believe taking a season to explore more intentionally can be healthy for some. But if you are resisting opportunities to grow or opting out of the hard things in life because you want to go live on a yacht, I think it's time for a change.

# Get the [F]ear out of Your Head

Today's challenge:

1.  Take some time to write a vision for your life. Where do you see yourself in five years? What do you ultimately want out of life; marriage, kids, a business, a good church, a house by the beach? Be specific with what you want and see in your future.
2.  Set goals to achieve this vision, including making a budget. Begin to invest in your future by listening and reading resources from those who have found success in those areas.
3.  Start saying no to short term adventures that don't align with your vision. Commit **to an area of serving your church or community. Be someone who is dependable because you are brave enough to stick around.** Shake that fear of settling down by putting down some roots!

# FEAR OF
# GOING UNNOTICED

Many of our fears aren't always a product of our experiences, but rather are born out of our deepest insecurities. As this fear begins to consume our thinking, we often project what we are feeling onto other people. This can lead to assuming they are treating us the same awful way we are treating ourselves. Although we don't realize it. In some cases, people may actually begin to take advantage of you, whether by ill intent or simply because you turn yourself into a doormat for them. The fear of going unnoticed is one that I have lived out for far too long, and I don't want you to have to go through the same pain.

Have you ever been in a room full of influential people and asked yourself what the heck you are doing in that room? I've had that feeling one too many times, and I think it's possibly one of the most intimidating feelings of insignificance we can think about ourselves. People who carry authority, position, and power are admirable, no doubt.

But we should never equate someone's position or status as what they are worth or a measurement that we cannot attain. Instead, we should look to them as a reference point for what is possible and learn from their life to achieve that same level of greatness.

There was a time in my life when I really felt unaccomplished and overlooked in every area possible. I had been a nanny for about seven years at the time and was tired of helping to raise other people's kids. I felt unnoticed in my love life, my calling to ministry, and my occupation. I even felt I had wasted seven years in a profession that was not impressive on my resume. It was an overwhelming feeling, and I decided to call it quits on my nanny career. I folded my proverbial Mary Poppins umbrella and got a job as a Catering and Marketing director at my friend's restaurant. This is really just a cool way of saying I sold sandwiches for a living. Yep, I hit an all-time low. During this time, I faced one of the darkest seasons in my life. Yet, ultimately, it brought me to a powerful awakening moment that eventually led me back to nannying. God showed me something very significant in that season: **no title, position, or job can offer you authentic significance in life. You will only find that sense of significance when you know who you are in Christ and live out of a whole heart that is secure in Him.**

1Peter 2:19 sets us straight: *"But you are God's chosen treasure—priests who are kings, a spiritual "nation" set apart as God's devoted ones. He called you out of darkness to experience his marvelous light, and now he claims you as his very own. He did this so that you would broadcast his glorious wonders throughout the world"* (The Passion Translation). This is how God sees us, as a treasure, set apart for His glorious wonders. We won't be able to be His glorious wonders messengers if we constantly view ourselves as the outcasts or last ones picked. It's time we get a shot of confidence in our veins, pull our shoulders back, and walk in the authority He has given us. God sees you, He notices you and that should be enough to make you feel like the most important person in the world.

## Get the [F]ear out of Your Head

Today's challenge:

1. Do you struggle with feeling under-appreciated, overlooked, or unnoticed? Do you always seek to get the credit with projects or your good ideas? Check your heart and examine the value systems you have created. What are you trying to measure up to?
2. Make a list of "I Am" statements and recite them every morning. Ask Jesus to help you anchor your identity in what He says about you.
3. When you're around influential people, don't give in to feelings of insignificance. You are just as important and valuable. Remember, you are a glorious wonder messenger-- don't allow intimidation to limit this gift!

FEARLESS CO.

"Your calling and your
destiny is weighty, as
it should be. But that's
the whole purpose of
it. God would never
allow you to feel
heaviness to let you
be discouraged. It's a
reminder for you to
see that your destiny
is a big deal."

KYMBER MARTIN

fearless.co_ • Following

fearless.co_ Shame is not your story.
Loved Kymber's episode of being an
influence in a tough industry and also
opening up about the liberation only an
everlasting Love can bring.

37w

nightsofunity 🔥 🔥 🔥
37w  2 likes  Reply

nicoletarpoff 🙌 🤍 ✨ 🔥
37w  2 likes  Reply

natalie_lemas @nikki.wierschem
@vanecalidonio @emma.burbie
37w  5 likes  Reply

Liked by estessss and 232 others

MARCH 14

Add a comment...                    Post

# FEAR OF HAVING FAITH

Most people assume that faith is a mere acknowledgement that God exists. But that's really not the true definition or experience of faith. Sure, it's a great place to start, but faith is a total reliance, dependence, and surrender to the love of God. It is an activator of our relationship that completely changes our human experience. Faith is the letting go of our limited understanding that cannot solve the equation of time and a complete embracing of a God who designed us and our world intelligently and with purpose.

The scary thing about faith is that it can almost feel wrong. Having faith can almost feel foolish, reckless, and even dangerous. When we step out in faith, our minds want to rationalize everything and convince us to run from the danger of entering the unknown. But that intimidating zone of uncharted territory is exactly where we need to be in order for faith to have its full effect in our lives. When we have nothing to cling to, our decisions seem irrational, and we look like an idiot for giving something away or saying yes to something far too big for us to handle-- this is when our faith is in full effect. It's in this space where an intimate relationship with your loving Creator is initiated and changes your entire trajectory on life.

I used to think I had a lot of faith because I grew up in a Christian family. I thought it was the kind of thing that just accrued over time, but I was wrong. Though I have had faith in God my whole life, I am only just now understanding how to truly have faith like Jesus.

Jesus loved big, without judgement, and without always having all the blanks filled in. In fact, most of the time, we see Jesus interacting with people who we probably wouldn't picture a Christian dude hanging with: prostitutes, adulterers, liars, thieves, and pretty much everyone who wasn't considered religious. Everything that Jesus did to walk out his faith was radical and an uncommon expression of love. The faith that Jesus had was unshakable, immovable, and totally confident that his father in heaven would act on His behalf.

Having faith is the complete opposite of living for the world. Faith requires some kind of lack or void or impossible situation. In fact, the Bible says it is impossible to please God without faith (Hebrews 11:6). **I believe God craves to be invited into your impossible situations by your faith. He looks at your pain, heartache, or your sickness and longs for you to reach out to Him with your faith**. But here's the kicker: He won't unless you do.

No matter how afraid you are of having faith, at some point, you are going to have to take the leap. There are times when I am not 100% sure that I am doing it right, but I do know I am taking steps in the right direction by simply inviting God to do what only He can do. Whether I falter along the way, I know that He will always pick me up and guide me to every right place. That is the assurance we can have when we have faith. It is an unexplainable assurance that somehow, someway, God is at work on our behalf, leading and guiding us into a better future. Having faith is worth the leap.

## Get the [F]ear out of Your Head

Today's challenge:

1. Maybe you grew up in church and have strayed away in recent years, due to a lack of connection. Or perhaps you were never religious and are only just now beginning to develop your faith. Regardless of where you are on the journey, God wants to have a real relationship with you, and that all begins with faith.

2. Faith isn't something you strive for. It is a place of rest; allowing God to be God, and waiting on Him. What are you believing God for? Write out a prayer to God releasing the thing you are believing Him for. Begin to confess every day, "God, I trust you with this. My faith is at rest in you." There is nothing you can do to earn God's love or His provision. All you must do is simply believe and have faith that He will do it.

FEARLESS CO.

WE ARE ALL CALLED TO
SO MANY STUNNING THINGS
IN LIFE, TIMES THAT ARE
FAR BIGGER THAN
ANYTHING WE CAN
EVEN IMAGINE,
MOMENTS THAT WILL
BE SEEN BY MANY AND
MILLIONS THAT WILL
NEVER BE SEEN BY
ANYONE OTHER THAN HIM.

SARAH LITTLE

fearless.co_ • Following

fearless.co_ What we see as ordinary, He sees as holy. Let us never under estimate the unseen moments. | blog post in bio

42w

ebiehepworth Boooooom

42w   Reply

jenn.louise.w 🫶 🫶

42w   Reply

taylornume Yessssss 🙌🙌🙌

41w   Reply

jenn__mcdonald You're my hero

Liked by estessss and **172 others**

FEBRUARY 12

Add a comment...                    Post

# FEAR OF MAKING WRONG DECISIONS

Have you ever been driving, following a GPS, and you get to a turnabout and flip your phone upside down to check every angle, trying to figure out which turn you're supposed to make out of the four options given? Asking for a friend. Through my personal experience in making decisions, I've found that life is full of turnabouts.

One time while I was in Australia, I was driving a caravan full of kids and accidentally went the wrong way around a turnabout-- meaning I was driving AGAINST traffic. Mind you, it was my first time driving on the opposite side of the road, so not only did I not know which turn to take, I got so disoriented I ended up having to dodge cars driving towards me before I finagled my way out. All the while, the little Aussie children were screaming bloody hell in the backseat. It was quite an exhilarating experience, and I may have given myself a hernia from all the anxiety it caused, but I eventually found my way! Praise God!

Sometimes, decisions in life can feel this way. We arrive at a point where we get to choose which way we will go. Sometimes the options are clear; other times, it feels like spinning in circles to find your way. Do you stay and get planted, or go and travel, or go find a new home? Do you date the guy and find out if it's worth it, or walk away now? Do you marry the man of your dreams and start a family, or break off the engagement? Do you start the business, or wait for another opportunity? The turnabout options are endless, and if we're not careful, we will find ourselves driving in circles into oncoming traffic and create a chaotic mess.

The good news is: your life GPS is way better than Google maps. Jesus offers us His Spirit in the form of a companion, a best friend and a guide. *"I will ask the Father and he will give you another Savior, the Holy Spirit of Truth, who will be to you a friend just like me—and he will never leave you,"* (John 14:16-17, TPT)

**We are not alone in making decisions.** And I have even better news. Even if you make the wrong turn, He will lead you back to the turnabout and keep guiding you until you're right where you're supposed to be. The Holy Spirit never abandons you. His GPS guiding service doesn't stop working even in remote scary places. I'm telling you, heaven's got software that would make Apple jealous. At times it may feel frustrating like you can't find clarity in the season of making a decision. And that's ok. He's not in a rush, so don't let those around you set your pace. Move with peace and trust that even when things feel motionless, He's working behind the scenes to guide you and make the signs so very clear. If you miss those signs, He's sending construction workers to create a detour, and if you're still that hard-headed, He's sending an old granny to the crosswalk to direct you with her cane, and if you're still lost he's sending police officers with a private escort to get you back to the turnabout, and on to where you're supposed to be.

Jesus is all about coming after the one who has strayed away and bringing them back to where they belong. So, don't be frustrated if you've looped that grassy middle garden a couple of times. Take your time. Enjoy the garden from every angle. Turn up the volume on your Holy Spirit GPS. Get in His Word. Pump up the worship. And I'm telling you the more you focus on His presence, rather than chasing your ambitions, the route you're meant to take will become so internally defined in you that you'll be smacking that indicator blinker without even realizing it and that turn will feel so natural, even a Justin Beiber fan club riot couldn't phase you. It's ok. You're going to be ok. You're equipped to make good decisions. I'm in it with you, and I have a feeling we're going to make it.

## Get the [F]ear out of Your Head

Today's challenge:

1. Do you often feel indecisive about your future? Do you constantly need affirmation from others to feel confident you made the right choice? Write down the decisions you are feeling uncertain of and begin to pray about them daily. Instead of worrying about them, thank God for guiding you and begin to focus on His presence more than the decisions.
2. Give yourself some time to breathe and remove the pressure from feeling like you have to make a decision now. If your thoughts start becoming anxious, begin to praise and thank God for leading you.

# FEAR OF FOLLOWING THE CALL OF GOD

I recently went through a season where I was wrestling with my decision to continue living in California, thousands of miles away from my family. The most valuable thing in life is found in relationships, especially family relationships, so why would I be compelled to live apart from the people who I love the most? I wish I had a solid answer and a simple solution to respond with. But what I've learned in this process is following the call of God on your life, and trusting in His purposes is never a simple or a one-dimensional experience. I find it to be a process of maturing and a constant act of surrender.

**God often places us in unknown, unfamiliar, and distant places to allow the uncertain mystery of life to fill the space in between our faith and His provision.** Like a canyon valley cliff, He stands on the other side as I gaze at the chasm below. With a smirk on his face, he extends his arms, motioning to join Him on the other side-- "*Come on, baby girl, take the leap.*" I stand alone. What is He thinking?! This is crazy. This doesn't make sense. But even from afar, I can see a look in His eyes. It's a look of wild wonder, like He can't wait to show me a surprise. I stand on the edge of the cliff, close my eyes, and take the leap. At first, it feels like a suicidal plunge. The feeling of uncertainty is all-consuming and doubts flood in like an ocean, interrogating my convictions. And though I may feel exposed to harm in this vulnerable space, it is undoubtedly the most powerful place I could be, submitting my will to the authority of Christ.

Though the feeling is scary, faith fills in the gaps. Yes, *faith is the only real thing you have in the midst of the leap, and you find it there better than you would standing on solid ground.* Faith doesn't feel. Faith just speaks and does and waits until our feelings catch up. So, you trust as the leaping goes on. Sometimes for longer than you imagined. But all the while you know you'll make it to the other side, because **God would never call you into something to abandon you, torment you, or disappoint you.** He gives you the opportunity to be courageous as you trust Him to guide you into His promises.

The wrestling really isn't between me and a geographical location. It is between me and my calling. As much as I love my family, and those God has placed in my life, my calling, where God takes me, and what He wants to do with my life is between me and Him. And while I believe God wants us to honor our families, and be fully present, He has also given us a command to be obedient to the unique call on our lives.

I have some friends who would never consider moving, simply because they are afraid of leaving their families, and living on their own. While I understand their concerns, I find it more concerning they may never hear God call them somewhere beyond their comfort zones because they aren't open to dreaming into it and letting go of what is familiar.

When you are obedient to the call of God on your life, He takes you places you never imagined you'd be. But this process always begins with a willing heart to go and do whatever He may ask. God will always provide what you need, including looking after your family and fulfilling the desires of your heart to be close to them. In my 7 years living apart from my family, God has provided ways for me to either come home to visit them multiple times a year or bring them out to me. Not only that, but my relationships actually got better as we became intentional about investing in each other no matter the distance. When you are faithful to the call, God will faithfully look after you.

## Get the [F]ear out of Your Head

Today's challenge:

1.  Have you been wrestling with your calling? Have you been afraid it would separate you from what you love most? This fear is an indicator that God is reaching out to you, waiting for you to take the leap. Journal today about what you're feeling and ask Jesus to give you the courage to take the leap.

# FEAR OF TRANSITIONS

"Gosh, I just love transitions and how painful they are. It just gives me goosebumps and makes me feel alive," said no one EVER! If you actually enjoy transitions, I'm sorry, but I'm going to need you to put the book down and slowly walk away, YUH WEIRDO! Just kidding, but on the real, transitions can be painful even when they lead to exciting new beginnings like becoming a new parent, getting married, or starting a new job. There are some transitions in life that will take you by surprise, and you will find yourself in a place where there is more gray than black and white; the unknown is all that lies before you, and all you are able to navigate is one tiny step at a time. These are the kind of transitions I'd like to remind you not to give up as you are making your way into a new place in life.

See, I'm in the middle of a transition myself. Currently,

my car is packed with all my belongings after I drove across the country from California to Florida to pursue my next steps. I moved out on one word from God and a vision He gave me for this season. Although it is still a bit fuzzy, I have learned that any transition is an invitation into deeper intimacy with Jesus. Sometimes, we have to let go of a few things we love in order to hold them again with a bigger heart. Remember, your story is still being written.

I read this verse in John 16:20-21 that knocked my socks off: *"...But know this, your sadness will turn into joy when you see me again! Just like a woman giving birth experiences intense labor pains in delivering her baby, yet after the child is born she quickly forgets what she went through because of the overwhelming joy of knowing that a new baby has been born into the world"* (The Passion Translation, 2017.).

Now, I don't know about you, but I personally have never birthed another human being. However, I get the picture Jesus was painting for us. (Thanks for the graphic image, Jesus). Transitional labor is a specific time between active labor and the actual delivery of the baby. It's this really awkward in-between time where a lot of pain is happening, but nothing can be done to speed up the process. Sometimes a waiting period that is so painful can feel extremely useless as if nothing is happening. But the truth is, the pain you're experiencing as a result of transition is evidence of the promise making its way to you. This is not a time for you to be cluttering your life with business and trying to make stuff happen. **This transitional season is designed for you to rest, lean into what God is saying, spend time with Him, and allow Him to reveal each step to you one at a time.** God can do far more with your faith at rest in Him than He can with a thousand attempts to make it happen energized by fear.

# Get the [F]ear out of Your Head

Today's challenge:

1. SLOW DOWN.
2. Be thankful for how far you've come.
3. Spend time with God and ask Him to re-imagine your future with you.
4. Write down one thing you are most afraid of about this season of transition and then write the opposite, i.e. "I'm afraid of losing all my friends," turns into, "I will not lose any friends because my friends love me no matter the distance." **Recite this out loud daily until you kick this fear in the butt!**

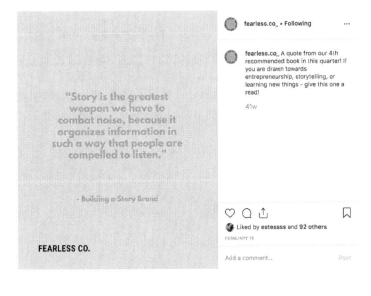

fearless.co_ • Following

fearless.co_ A quote from our 4th recommended book in this quarter! If you are drawn towards entrepreneurship, storytelling, or learning new things - give this one a read!

41w

"Story is the greatest weapon we have to combat noise, because it organizes information in such a way that people are compelled to listen."

- Building a Story Brand

FEARLESS CO.

Liked by estessss and 92 others

FEBRUARY 16

Add a comment...                    Post

# FEAR OF
# BEING WEAK

In order to define what it looks like to overcome the fear of being weak, I believe it's first necessary to re-define what being strong looks like. Most people associate strength with physical or mental ability to endure heavy things, literally and figuratively. When someone is in a lot of pain but seems to be keeping it all together, we often call them strong. We've defined strength as an attribute of someone who shows no emotions, doesn't break under pressure, and is capable of enduring pain unphased. But I would like to propose that true strength goes far deeper than our surface-level concept.

A few years ago, I wrote an article for an online publication on my definition of strength. This is an excerpt from the article:

*"Strong is attractive. It's not a sex-appeal based on what can be seen; it's built-in power within. Strong is the confidence to see the attainable possibilities beyond what is physical.*

*Strong is not perfect skin; it's visible muscles and invisible fortitude. Strong is bended knees of surrender. Strong is a fervent prayer. Strong is a smile through the hard times. Strong is not how you look, but how you look at others. Strong does not see others as weak but is always willing to lend its strength. Strong is discipline. Strong is not being afraid to fail but also not being afraid to succeed. Strong is the extra mile after exhaustion has set in. Strong is blood, sweat,and tears- blood for when life blindsides you with a paralyzing blow, sweat for the exertion of reserved energy to fight back with determined force, tears for when a grateful heart celebrates a victorious end. Strong is vulnerability at the risk of being harmed. **Strong is weakness reborn."***

I believe these words with all my heart. When we allow ourselves to be weak, we allow strength to be born in the vulnerable moments of life. There is no need to force yourself to have it all together for fear that others will assume you are weak. In fact, there's a scripture in 2 Corinthians 12:9-10 that actually reveals how powerful our weaknesses are: *"...My grace is sufficient for you, for my power is made perfect in weakness. Therefore **I will boast all the more gladly about my weaknesses**, so that Christ's power may rest on me. That is why, for Christ's sake, I delight in weaknesses, in insults, in hardships, in persecutions, in difficulties. For when I am weak, then I am strong"* (TPT). How dynamic is that? The writer of Corinthians flips the script and actually brags about being weak because he knows true strength is found in allowing God to fill in the gaps. This is a mindset that will change our lives if we begin to rewire our thoughts not to be ashamed of weakness, but begin to embrace it.

# Get the [F]ear out of Your Head

Today's challenge:

1.  What areas in your life do you feel are most weak? Write these down and reflect on how you feel about these weaknesses. Do they make you feel insecure? Do they make you feel incapable or exposed? Do you compare yourself to others who have this strength?

2.  Have a conversation with Jesus about how you can begin to allow His power to fill in the gaps of your weaknesses. God wants to turn your weaknesses into strengths, but first, He wants you to be vulnerable, admit you have weaknesses, and give you a safe place to rest and find strength in allowing Him to carry you through.

# FEAR OF
# HAVING HOPE

When disappointment hits us like a flood, it can often feel impossible to have hope again for the thing you desired. In fact, having hope is terrifying because you make yourself vulnerable to the chance of being disappointed again. In extreme cases, we often resort to a self talk to convince ourselves we don't want the thing we felt was either denied to us or never transpired.

Sometimes our problems in life can feel so dark it seems impossible to have hope and see the light at the end of the tunnel. Even worse, a difficult season can last so long that we begin to grow accustomed to disappointments and even find comfort in it. Eventually, we become numb and hold no expectations and actually become afraid of having hope. Weary from the constant let downs, we adopt the belief that "it is what it is," and no longer look for the light of hope. We shove our dreams under the bed and brush them aside as if we are doing ourselves a favor by alleviating the pressure of expecting what could be but isn't.

As vulnerable as it can be to have hope again, it actually has the potential to bring healing and wholeness to your heart in a powerful way. With hope, we can go through hard times with an outlook that truly believes good things are to come and ditch the cynical or apathetic view. Hope fills us with confidence to get through the hard times with the comfort of knowing this is not the end. It also offers us courage to dream again and re-imagine what God could do, even in a hopeless situation.

I'm not talking about the wishful thinking kind of hope. I'm talking about an anchor for your soul kind of hope, that even when the odds are stacked against you and everyone says it's impossible, you can't be convinced otherwise.

There is a story in the Bible about a couple named Abraham and Sara. God promised Abraham that He would be a father, but Abraham was pushing one hundred, and Sara's internal clock was tickin'! But, God chose them as the perfect candidates for His promise to be fulfilled. Why? It appears God is a huge fan of impossibilities and choosing underdogs for His favorite missions. When God spoke to Abraham about having a son, you'd think the miracle worker would get the ball rolling right away. Nope. God didn't fulfill His promise to Abraham for another twenty-five years! Can you imagine Sara taking a pregnancy test and it appearing negative time after time? (Ok, I know they probably didn't have pregnancy tests back then, but work with me here.) Can you imagine the heartbreak and disappointment year after year? They even tried the whole surrogate mother deal, yet that wasn't God's plan for them. Still, Abraham clung to hope by faith, expectant that God would fulfill His promise. And twenty-five years later, God came through. Why? Was God waiting for Abraham to get enough faith? No, that would have required striving and an earning of blessings mentality, but that's not God's way of doing things. Instead, I believe

God had us in mind with Abraham's journey. I believe God specifically planned out the timeline for when He was going to fulfill His promise to Abraham and Sara and allowed the journey to be as long and impossible as it was because it created the perfect scenario for a miracle, for God to do what only He could do.

The Bible says faith is the only evidence we need for the things God has promised, even if they are unseen. Now that is true hope when your heart is longing for a promise, yet your joy is satisfied in the promise keeper because you know He is faithful.

## Get the [F]ear out of Your Head

Today's challenge:

1. Have you allowed the light of hope to die in your heart? Have you convinced yourself you no longer want what you used to hope for because you believe it's just not going to happen, and that's just the way it is? Begin to journal about these things and don't hold back.

2. Hebrews 10:23 says, *"Let us hold unswervingly to the hope we profess, for he who promised is faithful."* Anchor your hope in the faithful one today. Have a conversation with Jesus about the areas you have felt disappointed in and allow Him to breathe life back into them. God wants to show Himself faithful to you.

# FEAR OF STARTING

I read a quote by Amy Poehler today that rocked me to my core, *"Great people do things before they are ready."* This both stung and got me fired up! I can't tell you how many times I have done things that were so far outside of my comfort zone and produced positive, life-changing results, yet I never once felt 'ready' to do them. I have found that most often we don't start things, not only because we don't feel ready, but because we don't know how to finish them. This mindset can affect many areas of our lives and hijack our dreams, causing us to live in a constant revolving door of never quite moving forward with an idea or desire. I experienced this several years ago when I had just started surfing and to be honest, I wasn't very good. Though I wanted to get better, I knew I wouldn't have the drive to improve unless I put a little pressure on myself. So in an impulsive effort to go for the big leagues, I signed up for a surf contest, and had four months to prepare!

The day of my contest I was sweating bullets, I was so nervous. A few minutes before my heat (my timeslot to compete), my friend turned to me and said, "Are you ready?" I stared out on the wild waves that looked like monsters crashing to the shore, looked back at her, and said, "Not at all." I had spent months preparing for this competition and daydreamed about what that moment would feel like. Yet, no matter how much I practiced, I still didn't *feel* ready. The reality was I felt afraid, anxious, and a little nauseous, to be honest. I had two options: back out of the heat and use the excuse of not feeling ready, or face my fear, get out of my comfort zone, and do it anyway. Thankfully, I chose the latter option and paddled out into my heat, completely terrified, yet faking it as best as possible to keep a cool head. I think I caught one and a half waves and placed fourth out of five contestants and, believe it or not; I was super proud of how I did! I may not have been the best surfer, but in the face of my fear, I was the bravest!

I love that I didn't ask anyone's permission to sign up for this contest or think I needed to qualify according to a certain standard of skill sets or experience. I simply chose to start the journey to do my best, even if that meant coming in last place, it didn't matter. What mattered is that I showed up and went for it.

No matter how much time you spend in preparation, launching into something new is scary, and you will most likely never fully *feel* ready. But just because you don't *feel* ready, doesn't mean you *aren't* ready. **If we wait for perfect conditions to take action, we will never get anything done.** Confidence comes from doing. Once you step out into that new thing, you will find a confidence that empowers you to achieve your dreams. You don't have to be the best right away. Start where you are and be brave enough to show up and go for it.

## Get the [F]ear out of Your Head

Today's challenge:

1. Are you afraid of starting something? Don't worry; you can do this! Don't run from your moment; it's time to show up. Make one decision right now that will lock you into taking the next step. Maybe it's submitting an application, making a phone call, or starting that business! Whatever it is, take action now whether you feel like it or not!

2. Take the practical steps to prepare yourself to do your best. Map out a plan, meet with a mentor, and ask a friend to hold you accountable. Give yourself time and grace to learn, develop, and grow. But when the moment comes to start, be brave and take a leap of faith! **Choose to BE ready and the confidence will eventually follow.**

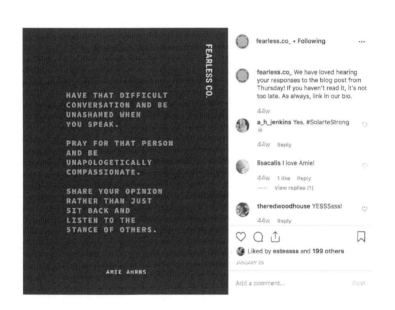

FEARLESS CO.

HAVE THAT DIFFICULT
CONVERSATION AND BE
UNASHAMED WHEN
YOU SPEAK.

PRAY FOR THAT PERSON
AND BE
UNAPOLOGETICALLY
COMPASSIONATE.

SHARE YOUR OPINION
RATHER THAN JUST
SIT BACK AND
LISTEN TO THE
STANCE OF OTHERS.

AMIE AHRNS

fearless.co_ • Following                    ...

fearless.co_ We have loved hearing
your responses to the blog post from
Thursday! If you haven't read it, it's not
too late. As always, link in our bio.

44w

a_h_jenkins Yes. #SolarteStrong

44w    Reply

lisacalis I love Amie!

44w    1 like    Reply
····· View replies (1)

theredwoodhouse YESSSsss!

44w    Reply

Liked by estessss and **199 others**

JANUARY 25

Add a comment...                     Post

# FEAR OF
# NOT FITTING IN

When you are new to a group, fitting in can be a challenge. You want people to accept you for who you are. You want to freely be yourself. But sometimes it's not that easy. Being the new kid can be intimidating, and often, the fear of fitting in can cause us to give in to peer pressure or social anxiety and cause us to act like someone we aren't.

There have been times in my life when I was afraid I wouldn't fit into a new community, and to be honest, in the end, I found I actually just didn't. Not because anything was wrong with me or the group of people, but just because I truly was in that group for just a season and fitting in would have caused me to settle in and not continue on the journey. When I look back on all of those groups of friends and communities and how hard I tried to be liked by them, get invited to all of the events, or simply feel comfortable around them, I laugh at all my striving. Though I had the right intent, I wish I could go back, shake myself and say, "Homegirl, get it together! Stop trying to lower your standard of friendship. You belong in a community of greatness!" If only I knew then how God would one day place me in a community of people who challenge my calling, cheer me on in my dreams, and draw out the best in me to be the best person I can be and love Jesus with everything I have. I wish I would have stopped trying to fit in and been a thermostat in those groups, rather than a thermometer, always trying to adapt to how others lived.

Acceptance is something we all desire, but fitting in doesn't mean you have to blend into the crowd. You can actually be yourself, stand out, and still be accepted. It's important to know this for ourselves and not search for approval from others. The cornerstone to our confidence should be in the truth that God accepts us and made us perfectly just as we are. The Bible says that you are God's unique creation (Psalm 139:13-14). You don't have to act like anyone else to fit in. You were BORN to stand out and be all that you are, without fear of judgment, or lack of support from your friend, group, or community.

The fear of fitting in diminishes who we truly are. Not only does it hinder our personality, but it can also cause us to run from new opportunities out of fear of rejection. Sometimes, we disqualify ourselves from participating because we are intimidated by others and how they may judge us. This is a lie that holds you back from entering in, making new friends, and enjoying an experience that you could love. Don't exclude yourself by opting out of opportunities to connect. But also, don't force yourself to stay in a community you know aren't your people. Be secure in who you are and know God has a community for you that will build you up and help you achieve your fullest potential.

# Get the [F]ear out of Your Head

Today's challenge:

1. Are you feeling lonely for authentic community, and like you have been forcing yourself to fit in where you are? God may have you in your community for a season But don't let yourself blend in. Be a thermostat in the group and lead by example. Set the standard for what a true friend is, and the values you want to live by. Stand by them with conviction and love others, even if they disagree.

2. Continue to pray for God to send opportunities your way to make authentic connections and find a community of people who share the same values as you. Look into church groups, community sports, or consider taking up a new hobby or serving at church to put yourself in environments around people who may share common interests and values.

FEARLESS CO.

In marriage when we celebrate each other's quirks, gifts, an dreams, it becomes a beautiful symphony of a safe place. It's only in a safe place that real connection is nurtured.

ZAC HEPWORTH

fearless.co_ • Following
Boise, Idaho

fearless.co_ Wow! We got more feedback on yesterday's podcast than ever before. Y'all LOVE @zachepworth and all that he has to say about marriage. Drop your favorite part below!

30w

alyssakenyon @red_alerts @renaenae1813 @cassijean_

30w    2 likes    Reply

ally.m.smith Truth BOMBS

30w    1 like    Reply

jaimiann I loved the practical application to talking about each

Liked by estessss and 219 others

MAY 2

Add a comment...    Post

# FEAR OF NOT BEING FOUGHT FOR

My spirit animal must be a lion because there is nothing tame or safe about the way my heart leads me to live. When I see people in need, my heart is eager to rescue. I don't hold back with reserve, and I wear my heart on my sleeve, unashamed, to the world. But what this wild heart of mine didn't realize, was that much of my impulsive nature was an excessive expression of insecurity I covered up.

There is a quote from the book Wild at Heart by John and Stasi Eldridge that had me spinning in my chair, *"When Eve was deceived, the artistry of being a woman took a fateful dive into the barren places of control and loneliness. Now every daughter of Eve wants to control her surroundings, her relationships, her God. No longer is she vulnerable, now she will be grasping.* **No longer does she want simply to share in the adventure, now she wants to control it***. And as for her beauty, she either hides it in fear and anger or she uses it to secure her place in the world.* **Her fear that no one will speak on her behalf or protect her or fight for her** *(causes her) to recreate both herself and her role in the story. She manipulates her surroundings so she doesn't feel so defenseless. Fallen Eve either* *becomes rigid or clingy. **Put simply, Eve is no longer simply inviting. She is either hiding in busyness or demanding that Adam come through for her.***"

My jaw dropped to the floor in utter shock at the perfectly tailored description of my wounded heart. I had never known or seen certain traits I carried to be manipulative or controlling, but just the day before reading this, I had a conversation regarding how I made a guy feel pressured to pursue me. As I spent time praying about this, I realized that deep down I was afraid no one would fight for me, so I did everything in my power to prove my worth and try to fight for myself.

For years I was obsessed with controlling my relationships and afraid that no one would fight for me. In each one of these situations, I demanded Adam come through for me the superlative 21st century Eve. Well, in my most recent case, my manipulation worked...for a week and then it came crumbling down as I could hear God say, *"Let him go."* It's interesting how He does that, isn't it? Leads you through a door that you thought was an opportunity, but turns out was just a fire-escape route away from your pride.

As tears poured down my cheeks and mascara stained my shirt, I screamed with a whisper into my hands, **"Will *You* fight for me? Will You *fight* for me? Will You please fight *for me*?!"** I heard a voice say, "Open the bible app." So I did, and amazingly, though not shockingly, I found His reply in the verse of the day: *"The Lord himself will fight for you. You need only to stay calm"* (Exodus 14:14, NIV) ARE YOU KIDDING ME!!?? I jumped off the couch and wiped the tears of disappointment off my face. The Lord HIMSELF is fighting for me. He is pursuing me! **Not only is He fighting on my behalf, but He is fighting for my HEART!** I am worth pursuing because God is pursuing me.

Many girls (and guys) believe they aren't worth being fought for. Maybe it's because the people you trusted most haven't stood up for you or made you feel supported. Or perhaps it's because you have only ever surrounded yourself with passive relationships and never allowed people with strong integrity and values to come alongside you. Many times, this is due to our lack of trust in others and our fear of letting them close. But there is so much freedom found in knowing that God is on your side and is fighting for you every day!

## Get the [F]ear out of Your Head

Today's challenge:

1. Do you often find yourself trying to control or manipulate situations? Perhaps you are unaware of this and think you are just being nice when you go out of your way to make something happen. Search the motives in your heart and ask God to reveal to you if there are areas in your life you are trying to control.
2. Take time to examine the friendships in your life. Do these friendships make you feel fought for? How do you come alongside others? Do you make them feel fought for? Pray and ask God to put healthy relationships in your life, people who know your value, and who celebrate you.
3. God is fighting for you. Trust Him and begin to let down your walls to allow the right people in. Break old unhealthy habits and develop new ones out of a place of confidence knowing you are worth fighting for.

FEARLESS CO.

"The power of showing up takes effort and planning and perhaps will even cost something on my part. But in it, I will trust God that I will not only receive but I will contribute.

He is switching me from a consumer to a contributor through showing up and faithfully serving. Especially when it feels inconvenient."

**HANNAH CUSACK COWART**

fearless.co_ • Following

fearless.co_ @hcusackcowart droppin 🔥

36w

jkbarth WOW🏆🙌 needed this!!!

36w  Reply

121 likes

MARCH 21

Add a comment...                    Post

# FEAR OF LIVING YOUR PURPOSE

Do you ever find yourself daydreaming in your car in mid-traffic about quitting your job, selling everything, buying a Volkswagen bus, and hitting the road? No? Oh, I mean, yeah, me neither... Honestly, though, it seems like all my friends are going on extended road trips, backpacking across Europe, traveling wherever the wind blows, and living what we call 'the life.' But is it really?

Sure, I'll be honest, I'm a little jealous. But I've been wrestling with this idea for a while now. Everywhere I turn, people are on an endless quest for adventure. But will adventure and experiences alone satisfy us? I truly believe our desire for adventure is an external expression for a question echoing in our hearts: *What do we want in life?* From what I've gathered, some of the conclusions aren't as fulfilling as they appear. Some of the things we want don't bring us satisfaction. In fact, they create more questions and more searching. Our pining for more leads us into the wild, giving in to everything our heart desires. We want all of the extreme and none of the moderation. We want everything reckless and none of the boundaries. We want everything wild and nothing too safe. We want endless youth and non-committal responsibilities. We want to be alone and wander into the unknown, chasing flames of romance and bursts of dreams. We want to be famous but not fully known. We want to be carelessly rich and indulgent in plenty. The search, the quest, the pining after empty things lingers on: *What do we want in life?* I believe the answer we are looking for is found deeper than our desires, located in a place within our heart; not many are willing to navigate. Do we dare explore a landscape unsearchable with human eyes- the mountains within us no compass can navigate?

If we had the courage to dig deeper, we would find we long for truth. We want authenticity. We want to know what's real and what's really worth living for. We want love, the dangerous kind that believes impossible things can happen if you're willing to not give up; the untainted by human definition, organic, kind of love that makes you foolish like a bad rom-com. Not because you feel it, but because the presence of it is so tangible in your life, it's both undeniable and indescribable; the kind of love that takes your breath away and gives it back. We want this with each other, but also with the Eternal.

It's in this place I've come to realize what we truly want in life isn't easily cured by an adventurous escape or exhilarating experience. I've come to wonder if maybe the idea of constant travel is not so much the ultimate lifestyle as it is the ultimate fear of fulfilling our purpose. I believe many of us are afraid to discover that what we truly want is going to take hard work, commitment, and never giving up on that real kind of love. Many people run from living their purpose because they are afraid they either don't have one or don't know how to discover it. I want you to know, God created you with purpose *for* a purpose. God made everything with a divine design; nothing was created by mistake or without intention. **Your purpose isn't about what you were created for, but why you were created.** And the good news is, if you're feeling disconnected from this sense of purpose, all you have to do is ask God to reveal it to you.

Living life with a sense of purpose causes us to live each day with intention, not just randomly or spontaneously, as my travel junky friends do. Yet, there is nothing boring about this whatsoever. Every day is full of wonder as you allow your Creator to unveil His divine plan for your life and guide you in how to live out your purpose. Once you lock into your purpose, you won't be running from, but running *to* every opportunity to grow into the person God has called you to be.

## Get the [F]ear out of Your Head

Today's challenge:

1. Have you been living somewhat aimlessly and not giving much thought or vision to your life or future? Do you work at a job that just pays the bills but doesn't resonate with your passion? God wants to rekindle your purpose and help you redefine your idea of adventure.
2. Take time to write down a vision for your future and what you believe your purpose is. Include in your definition that your main purpose is to be a child of God and live in relationship with Him. Everything else comes after that. Make plans to start pursuing your purpose and enjoy the adventure!

# FEAR OF GROWING UP

I can remember it like it was yesterday, the good ole days when I was a kid, and my biggest concern in life was hoping I didn't get picked last for dodgeball. Back then, it felt like an eternity before I could be of an age worthy of staying up late or going to the mall alone with friends. But before I knew it, it's as if someone hit the fast forward button, and here we are today: an adult.

It can be a difficult transition from childhood into adulthood. It's a weird thought to realize we're not the only ones getting older; our parents, friends, nieces and nephews and kids we used to babysit are now graduating high school; all growing up, too. The way time moves, both slow and fast, is a mystery. Some days it feels like just yesterday we were kids climbing trees, yet it also feels like a distant dream.

When I turned twenty-five, I discovered a startling reality: I'm an adult! I have to make hard decisions by myself. I have to know, choose, and believe what's right. I have to wake up early and set an alarm clock and have no one to yell at me to get up, pay my bills, or go to work. These are responsibilities I alone am accountable for. What happened to the awesome idea of going to the mall without a chaperone?! I thought being an adult would be way more fun!

Maybe you can't relate, but as the youngest child in my family, I clung to my childhood like a little kid with a death grip on her favorite teddy. The reality of being an adult began to weigh down on me like a ton of bricks. Being responsible is hard and way less appealing than being taken care of at your parents' house. Anxiety filled my thoughts with every concept of fear of the future and caused me to spiral into a dark well of depression. What I didn't realize during this time was there is a process by which we mature and naturally grieve our childhood. I lost my motivation to pursue my dreams. I lost my sense of purpose and confidence in what I was called to do. Each day was a battle of anxiety attacks. All I wanted to do was sell everything I owned, move back in with my parents, and avoid the responsibilities of growing up. No worries, no bills, no responsibilities, and no pressures. But running from my fear wasn't going to get me anywhere. There was no denying I had to face this fear head-on. So I did. I stayed at my big girl job, worked diligently, and began to pursue my passions again. Four years later, it has brought me to a place of peace and dreams coming true that I only ever imagined.

The more I allowed myself to give in to the maturing process, the more comfort and confidence I found in being an adult and letting go of my childhood in a healthy way. I learned that **growing old is inevitable, but growing up is optional.** Not everyone makes the effort to mature and shed the old habits or mindsets from their childhood that limit them from growing as adults. But maturing is an essential part of life that helps us achieve our dreams. We can choose to stay afraid of the change growing up brings, or we can embrace it and mature as new responsibilities present themselves.

## Get the [F]ear out of Your Head

Today's challenge:

1. I challenge you to not run from the hard jobs, responsibilities, or pressure. Instead, face it by being strong and recognizing that your dreams can be fulfilled as you push forward. Don't disconnect from your passion. Pursue what makes you come alive and trust the process of growing up.

2. Ecclesiastes 3:1 says, *"There is a time for everything, and a season for every activity under the heavens."* If the season you are now in is adulthood, don't freak out, it's going to be good. Ask God to give you the confidence to let go of childish behaviors and embrace this season you are now in. Ask Him to show you anything in your life you have an unhealthy death grip on that is attached to trying to relive your childhood. Let Him speak into that and show you a new way of living.

*"We all need people in our lives who will tell us what we don't want to hear."*

- Adamant

FEARLESS CO.

fearless.co_ • Following

fearless.co_ Who's reading our quarterly recommended reads? Adamant is rocking our world. 🔥

35w

chelsealeekeller @lightlystitched so glad I have you!! This is so us we can speak to each other with love and intention knowing we have our best interest at heart!

35w 1 like Reply

—— View replies (1)

ohboymama_ Yes 🙌 🙌

35w Reply

hey.nicola.kay I got you

♡ ◯ ⬆ 🔖

Liked by estessss and 150 others

MARCH 30

Add a comment… Post

# FEAR OF SUCCESS

Success is something we all want to achieve, but there are times when the idea of success is scary. Many of us have big dreams, but when the realization of responsibility hits, or we imagine the pressure that comes with certain successes, we often pull back from achieving our dreams. At times, we even sabotage our success because we are so afraid we don't have what it takes.

You might have a dream to own a business, buy a house, go back to school, or start a family. These are all amazing ideas, but the reality is a lot of these dreams require intense paperwork, lots of money, serious contracts, and huge life shifts. Even writing this book was a daunting idea at the beginning, and even as I am finishing writing it, there is still the marketing and sales strategy I have to work towards, and the list goes on. Successes can often bring more problems, though many times we prayed for these problems.

There was a time when I was so afraid of achieving my dream of being a successful writer that I literally never told people I had published books. I would be in conversations with people, and when asked what I do, I completely blanked on the fact that I'm a writer. In fact, my friends would have to interject in these conversations and speak up for me. I felt tremendous pressure to meet the expectations of others and unattainable expectations I placed on myself. I knew I had everything in me to achieve my dreams, but the thought of it scared the crap out of me. This fear was a very real reality. I couldn't help but feel like if I was successful, it would mean I would have to show up and own up to the commitments I'd made. There's no reversing that and no hiding from life once you go all in. There's more responsibility, more influence, which creates less margin for mistakes. People will be counting on me, and that's scary. Not only that, but I was also afraid of how other people would perceive me when they saw me going full throttle after my dreams. Would they think I was conceited or trying too hard? What if they didn't take me seriously? Every possibility tormented me until I felt paralyzed.

The fear of success will eventually cause you to grow discouraged and give up on your dreams, though you may not even be aware. Excuses become your new normal as you try and convince yourself that you're "just not ready," and because of this, you may drop out of classes, step down from positions of leadership, or leave a promising job because things are starting to get REAL!

Yes, it's true, the success of our dreams will require responsibility, commitment, and sacrifice, but the rewards of pushing through the challenges are far better than running from what could be the greatest adventure of your life. Being afraid of success is only going to keep you stuck and cause you to hijack the natural process needed to develop your full potential. God designed you to flourish in your purpose. But you will only go as far as you allow yourself to. In Joshua 1:8, God reminds us the secret to success is found in knowing Him and following His perfect plan. We don't have to be afraid of success if we put our trust in God to lead and sustain us.

## Get the [F]ear out of Your Head

Today's challenge:

1. Have you backed off from certain areas of leadership that intimidated you? Does the idea of becoming influential and responsible make you cringe? Make note of the areas you struggle with and create a plan of action on how you can counteract your fear.
2. Write out a personal definition of what success looks like to you. Do the opposite of what your fear has trained you to do in the past. If you tend to keep quiet, speak up. If you let others lead, step forward. I believe in you!

# FEAR OF FEAR

*"The only thing we have to fear is...fear itself — nameless, unreasoning, unjustified terror which paralyzes needed efforts to convert retreat into advance."* This is a quote by President Franklin D. Roosevelt that he shared during his inauguration as president in 1933. His words are striking and powerful. Many of our fears are born out of the tension we create in our apprehensions toward life. A counselor once pointed out to me how I often brace myself for the worst and create problems in my head because I'm afraid of feeling the fear if it were to occur. It's not always the situation I'm afraid of, it's the feeling of fear itself that I dread.

This got me thinking, maybe we get so worked up over the idea that we're doing something wrong, or are not pleasing to our others because we are afraid that if we truly let our hearts run free, they will not measure up to the expectations put on us. So we allow the lies to build a storm in our head and create a traumatic fantasy as we brace ourselves for the worst.

We are afraid of letting people down. We are afraid of failure. We are afraid of discontent. We are afraid that we won't be happy. We are afraid of what we feel. We are afraid of being misguided. We are afraid we will compromise our dreams for a monotonous life. We are afraid of committing to the process. We are afraid the end result will not be satisfying. We are afraid that once we finally get what we want, then we won't want it anymore. We are afraid of getting bored in our relationships, in our jobs, in our settling down and creating roots. We are afraid of a God who we believe is going to force us to do something that makes us cringe, go somewhere we hate, or marry someone we aren't attracted to. We are lured into the wild and taken captive by an elusive desire for adventure, a perpetual hunt for a feeling that makes us feel somehow adequately human. Our concept of enough is unattainable. Pleasure is our drug. This is the struggle we face as we fear being afraid. However it may come, however it may present itself, we are constantly dealing with opportunities to learn how to overcome our fears and gain authority over our thoughts that seem to project our inner demons into reality.

As Joyce Meyer always says, "The mind is a battlefield." We need to recognize when we're under attack and be pro-active against the lies of fear before they ever make it into our reality. We need to learn how to be on guard and ready for combat. We also need to learn how to give ourselves a break and receive the grace of God to help us get through.

I once heard Pastor Bobbie Houston share a valuable piece of advice: "Let prayer do the heavy lifting." Maybe instead of trying so hard to figure it all out, what we need to do is let what we have, be enough for today, and trust God to do what only He can do. Though the process is often painful, there is so much authority to gain in these battles we face. But there is no rush to get it right overnight. Maybe we should take our focus off of the long-term goals we put so much pressure on ourselves to strive for-- relationship goals, career goals, family goals, travel goals-- and shift our focus to a more narrow view daily so see the bigger picture of what God is doing.

Joshua 1:9 says, *"Have I not commanded you? Be strong and courageous. Do not be afraid; do not be discouraged, for the LORD your God will be with you wherever you go"* (NIV). We don't have to fear the feeling of fear because God is with us. **Though fears may come, we can be empowered and encouraged to know the presence of God is enough to give us peace, protection, and a posture of victory in the midst of the battle.**

## Get the [F]ear out of Your Head

Today's challenge:

1. Chances are, there are areas in your life where you have projected your fear into situations that may not be entirely accurate. Take time to reflect on your life, relationships, and season. Consider the fears you've struggled with recently. Are you bracing yourself for the worst? Or do you see a hopeful solution?
2. Consider meeting with a counselor, or pastor to help you navigate the root of your fears and how to overcome them. There IS hope for you. There IS freedom. You won't have to live with this fear forever. You can be totally free from fear by the power of Jesus.
3. Take time to memorize Joshua 1:9 and speak it over the situations you are afraid of. God is with you in the middle of your storm or battle. You are not alone. He is fighting for you and giving you the victory.

# MY FEARLESS JOURNEY

Snow White sat alone in her parked 1974 Volkswagen Beetle. It was June of 2009, a sweltering hot summer day in southern Florida. Temperatures blazed into the mid-90s - typical Miami weather. Beads of sweat dripped down her back as she adjusted her wig and swung her feet out the car window. Yes, Snow White was a fraud. In fact, she was 18-year-old me, Esther Marie Gualtieri. At the time, I was working as a party Disney princess and had arrived at a 5-year-olds birthday party 30 minutes too early to walk in. Mind you, I didn't look a thing like Snow White, my wig was a frizz ball, and makeup was melting off my face, making me look more like the Grim Reaper than a Disney princess! Still somehow, I managed to get paid ten dollars an hour for the gig.

As I waited for the party to begin, I popped in a CD message from one of my new favorite speakers, Lisa Bevere. I had just recently learned about the injustice of Human Trafficking and had responded to an inner calling to bring freedom to those enslaved. It was through Lisa's organization that I made this discovery and immediately signed up to volunteer, so they sent me this CD in the mail and were a constant source of encouragement as I was learning how to navigate my calling.

I can remember the moment in my car like it was yesterday. Lisa's voice commanded with equal grace and authority as she spoke to my heart in a way I had never experienced. Her message was inspiring and brought me to tears as she prayed for everyone listening. She began to call out different gifts in those present at the gathering, and as she called them out, she had them repeat a prayer out loud to create a posture of willingness and obedience to whatever God may ask us to do.

No longer was I aware of my surroundings or the fact that I was a melting Disney princess. Tears rolled down my cheeks as I repeated these words after Lisa, "I will write the books, I will write the songs, I will declare the Word of God." Something powerful shifted beyond what I could explain. It was an awakening, and I felt free and empowered to do what I was destined for.

It's been eleven years, and during a recent interview, I recalled that Snow White moment that changed my life. It had been quite some time since I remembered that message and pivotal moment in my life. Recalling it sparked my curiosity to dig up Lisa's message. I listened intently as if it were the first time. In an instant, it seemed as if time had stopped when I heard her say, *"A gift lies dormant because of intimidation. But when you face what you fear, you become fearless."* My jaw dropped in pure shock. I had established Fearless.Co just three years prior, and our motto from the very beginning was: "Face your Fears, Achieve your Dreams." I had no clue back then how much of an impact those words would have on my life. But eleven years later, the words spoken over me that day have met me in my future. A seed was planted in my heart that would take years of watering before I could ever see the results. But

God knew, and I am forever grateful for Lisa for declaring them over me in my car that day.

Even before Fearless Co. was an existing business, God had a purpose for my life that was marked with fearlessness. Unbeknownst to me, I have been walking the fearless journey preparing for this very moment. Living this message out for myself has transformed my life and set me free in every way. It's been a process, not an overnight success. As I have been traversing through facing my own fears, I have been waiting for you. Yes, you are my dream come true. Your hands that grip the binding of a book that only existed in my imagination years ago - I dreamed of you holding it as you embarked on your own fearless journey.

My fearless journey has been marked with challenges and setbacks, doubts, and uncertainty. But in the midst of fighting my own battles and practicing what I preach, I was fighting for you and let me tell you, you are so worth fighting for.

I pray this message equips you to fight your own battles, not to run and hide from fear, but to face it head-on with a courageous heart. I pray you discover your purpose, find the freedom to dream again, and say yes to the adventures that await.

**Welcome to your fearless journey. It's a wild one**

# HOW FEARLESS CO. BEGAN

In 2012, I wrote my first book called <u>Twirling Skirts of Magic</u> to encourage little girls to change the world just by being themselves. In a rough draft of my book, I wrote the phrase "fearless girl with wings," and I fell in love with that name. That part of the story didn't make it into the final edit of my book, but I tucked that little phrase away. A few months after I published my book, I launched a blog and called it Fearless Girl. I blogged about facing fears and achieving dreams every week. During this time in my life, I had fallen in love with surfing and going on adventures. Yet, I knew very few girls who surfed and enjoyed adventuring as much as I did. Many of the activities I loved were male dominant and when I did come across another girl surfer, it always felt like a competition.

I continued surfing and going on adventures alone, until one day I met a girl on the beach. We immediately hit it off and became inseparable surf sisters. Through my friendship with Holly, I realized the massive need for a network of girls who could surf together, go on adventures, and have genuine community. Girls were feeling isolated, and like they had to compete in order to earn respect. I saw this as an opportunity to take the message written in my blog and use it as a way to unite and empower girls in my community. I started a website and Instagram account and began to reach out to girls, encouraging them to face their fears and achieve their dreams. Our community began to grow, meeting weekly for all kinds of adventures, and before we knew it, we were planning our first surf contest together as a fundraiser to raise awareness about human trafficking. During our event, we raised over $800 for two organizations and used our passion for adventure for the purpose of changing the world.

Six years later Fearless Girl has been re-branded into Fearless Co. to broaden our influence. As a business, we create powerful content to engage in conversation and see radical change. Over the years, we have reached thousands of girls around the world who are isolated and searching for significance. Our mission is to see a movement of underdogs rise up unhindered by fear, so they may live out their daring potential.

We have been able to make a measurable difference in our community, hosting events, inspirational surf clinics for women rescued from sex trafficking, speaking at local schools, and more!

# ANN MARIE'S STORY

When I think back on my childhood, I can remember it like it was yesterday, like an old black-and-white projector film: joyous times rolling down hills in barrels with my dad and hours of basketball in the driveway with my brother. I was so carefree and truly fearless.

When I became a teenager, insecurities started to emerge as my self- esteem plummeted. Adults who I thought would be there for me as an emotional support weren't there, especially my father. As disappointment after disappointment continued to hurt me, I started to look for ways to compensate for my lack of confidence. I turned to the easiest substitute- drinking alcohol. At the age of twelve, I got blackout drunk for the first time. I felt empty and resentful of anyone I had trusted, and drinking was the only thing that gave me a sense of control.

I wanted to stand out and be noticed by those adults who were missing in my life. I was shy, but I felt the urge to rebel to get the attention I craved. Because of my quiet nature, I chose to rebel the best way I knew how- with my appearance. I was enthralled with strong female figures like Joan of Arc. So, at the age of sixteen, I shaved my entire head and got my first tattoo. At that same time, I started dating a guy who was a skater and six years older than me. He soon became my whole world.

Since I couldn't get the loving connection I needed from my father, I turned to my boyfriend for validation. Every waking moment became about seeing my boyfriend and as a result, I lost all of my girlfriends. Our relationship lasted for seven years, and my life became a whirlwind of drinking, smoking pot, and experimenting with hallucinogens. I was all about shock value. I became promiscuous and experimented sexually. I couldn't be faithful in my relationships, mainly because I was always getting drunk. I was a mess and tried to hide it from the people who loved me the most. It wasn't long before the relationships in my family felt distant as I pushed everyone away to protect my personal sense of independence.

I knew I was living a life that my Catholic mother wouldn't approve of, and I lived with constant guilt because of it. She didn't even have to say a word for me to feel judged, and the guilt was tearing me apart. Instead of that guilt making me want to repent or change my ways, the judgment I felt made me want to rebel harder. The idea of religion and God made me feel uncomfortable. I felt like anyone who even uttered the word "Jesus" to me was in a cult and trying to convert me.

While I appeared to be a normal, working member of society during the week, I was dropping acid on the weekends. I struggled with intense anxiety attacks, constantly feeling like the walls were closing in on me. One day at work, I had an anxiety attack that was so bad I couldn't breathe or speak and felt completely paralyzed. All I could do was run outside to my car and call home. My dad picked up, and as I sobbed on the phone, he tried to calm me down. I remember in between sobs saying to him, "Dad, I feel so out of control. If I had a gun in my hand right now, I'd shoot myself in the head." I was desperate for freedom and relief, even desperate enough to take my own life. I was having a mental breakdown and didn't leave my house for a week after. Still, I was far from rock bottom.

I continued to dive deep into the bottomless pit of searching for fulfillment in alcohol and began to drink even more heavily. I was out of control! I can recall one occasion where I came into work so completely drunk that I couldn't even keep a straight face. Another time, at my coworker's bachelorette party, I drank so much that a police officer followed our limousine from the bar we had left to our friend's house. When the officer stopped us, he saw how drunk I was and demanded that my friends take me to the ER immediately.

That night at the ER, as I got my stomach pumped in an unfamiliar city, with no way home and friends who had left me, I had reached an all-time low. Yet still, this was not enough to wake me up. I was too afraid of leaving behind a lifestyle I knew all too well...a lifestyle that I thought defined who I was.

In an attempt to find a tangible sense of freedom, I took up surfing. I will never forget how it felt the first time I paddled out beyond the shore break and into the large, building waves. Everything was completely quiet, and a sense of absolute peace and joy filled my body, unlike anything I had ever felt before. When I caught my first wave, it was so freeing; I felt connected to God, something I had never experienced or even knew I longed for. From then on, surfing became my saving grace. It was the only thing that brought me peace and gave me hope. Although I was still struggling with anxiety, a momentous shift started to take place in my life as I pursued this newfound passion.

A few years into my surfing adventure, I came across a post on Facebook by Esther, founder of Fearless Girl (now Fearless Co.). I discovered she was promoting a surf contest to raise awareness about human trafficking, a huge problem that was affecting girls around the world, even right in my own community. I was shocked at this realization and decided to connect with Esther. She invited me to a Fearless Girl meeting at her house to discuss the contest. Although I was nervous about attending, I took the plunge and went to the meeting. When I made my way up the steps to the front door, I didn't know what to expect. I had a brief thought that I could still turn around and go home. But something inside pushed me to keep going. When I knocked on the door, Esther greeted me with a warm embrace, welcoming me into her home. As I sat in the meeting listening to Esther share about her passion to help girls rescued from human trafficking and use surfing as a platform to raise awareness, I was amazed at the opportunity to make a difference while using my passion to surf.

Esther was unlike anyone I had ever met before. Her love for God was so unthreatening and unassuming; it seemed like such a natural extension of who she was. It was the first time I didn't feel uncomfortable with the subject of Jesus, and I felt accepted. She shared openly about her faith in a tangible way, and it was the first time I truly saw God's pure light shining through someone. Her joyful personality and pure love for God had a huge impact on me.

That day, I decided to join the Fearless Girl mission and participate in the surf contest. I didn't realize at the time, but that moment was the beginning of my journey to true freedom. Through the community of Fearless Girl, I began to make significant relationships with other girls who were using their passion for surfing to help others in need. These girls were so encouraging and uplifting, and it quickly became a sisterhood for me, something I never had growing up. A change started to take shape in my life as the walls I had built up to keep people out began to come down.

I remember one early morning while surfing, Esther asked me about my faith. In between catching waves, we had a conversation that sparked an interest in me. I had closed the door to religion years ago and decided I didn't want to have anything to do with God. But something about the way Esther talked about her relationship with God made me want to know more. I started to see how God was working around me in other people's lives, and I had a desire to have that same relationship with Jesus.

The next week Esther invited me to a conference at her church. It had been ages since I had stepped foot in a church, and despite having an anxiety attack just before the conference, I mustered up enough courage to show up. I'll never forget that moment as the worship music played, and people began to lift their hands in surrender, tears streamed down my face. The tangible love of God was so real. I didn't feel judged or guilty like I had felt in the past. I felt accepted and for the first time, like I belonged. That night I said yes to Jesus and asked Him to be the savior of my life. I may not have understood it at the time, but all I know is the freedom I felt in that moment was greater than any wave I could have ever surfed!

I was elated to have experienced for myself what I had only assumed was exaggerated stories from my Christian friends growing up. Even though I was excited about this new experience, my journey was far from over. At the time, I had been taking antidepressants at the suggestion of my doctor. About a week after the conference that changed my life, I attended a Halloween party with a few friends. The party was packed with people. There was a half-pipe skate ramp in the backyard and rows of storage bins filled with mystery punch labeled according to alcohol strength. It was wild and crazy, but nothing uncommon from what I was used to. It didn't take long for me to jump right in and blend into the scene. At one point, someone started switching the labels on the punch. I had no idea what or how much I was drinking, and everything became a blur.

I arrived home late that night, completely drunk. Still, to this day, I have no recollection of what was going through my brain, but in a moment of poor judgement, I finally came face to face with rock bottom as I overdosed on a combination of antidepressants and hard liquor. A few hours later, my boyfriend woke up to me having a seizure, and he called 911.

I was in a coma for 24 hours while my family and boyfriend prayed for a miracle. When I came out of the coma at the hospital, it was the most surreal experience of my life. I could hear faraway voices as the doctors started to revive me. It felt like I was in the bottom of a dark well, and as I looked up, I could see a light guiding me out. In that moment, I felt like I was being reborn and instantly knew I was being given a second chance by God.

A few days later, Esther came to visit me while I was still in the hospital. I told her that experience served as a huge wake-up call and made me look at life differently. I was so aware that God was real and that I was alive for a reason.

I have now been sober for almost a year and am more confident and fearless than I have ever been in my life. I am proud to call myself a Christian, and I count my blessings every day. I have a supportive and loving family, wonderful friends, and a loving boyfriend. Most importantly, I have a relationship with Jesus Christ. He is with me through it all, and His love guides me to live my best life. I can humbly say I have become fearless because of the confidence that God has given me. When I look at myself now, I am astounded by how truly blessed I am. My identity is no longer in a relationship with a guy, how hard I party, or in trying to measure up to what other people think of me.

Sharing my story has been a daunting and truly vulnerable experience. The feelings associated with looking back on where you come from can be difficult, and revealing yourself to others can be scary. But I share it boldly, believing that my story will help another girl find the courage to pursue true freedom. I pray my journey inspires you to never give up, to break out of your comfort zone, to be liberated from the fear that holds you back from pursuing your best life, and finally, to be vulnerable with your story. I have learned that fear holds you back from doing what you know is right, from expressing yourself in your most genuine way, and from enjoying each day with complete satisfaction. That's not the kind of life anyone should live.

Just the simple fact that you are reading this book is a sign that you're searching for more. It's your first step toward true freedom. I'm so proud of you already and know you too can live free from fear.

You got this!
**xoxo,**
**Ann Marie**

# FEARLESS FAITH

We have one last secret to share on becoming fearless. It's called: having faith. Yes, without faith, fear will continue to have power over you. In Romans 10: 10 it says,

*"The heart that believes in him receives the gift of the righteousness of God—and then the mouth gives thanks[a] to salvation."*

Jesus died on the cross to save us from an empty and fear-filled life. Faith is our response to accept Jesus' invitation to an adventurous and full life. Faith means you are trusting in Jesus completely.

No matter how hard we work, we will never be able to withstand the power of fear on our own. We are also unable to wipe away our own shame or guilt that comes with living in sin. Only Jesus can take that away completely and gives us freedom and a fresh start.

If you want to experience this fearless faith, all you have to do is say yes to Jesus' invitation and start a relationship with Him. You can pray this simple prayer:

"God, I want to have fearless faith in you. I don't want fear to control my life any longer. Jesus, I ask you to take away my shame and give me a brand new start. I want to have a relationship with you and live an adventurous life, fearlessly with you. Thank you for answering my prayer, in Jesus name, Amen."

# UNHINDERED BY FEAR

## About The Author

**Esther Marie** is passionate about helping girls find freedom from fear to discover their true identity. Her extensive background in youth outreach, mentorship and anti-human trafficking initiatives led her to establish Fearless Girl (now known as Fearless.Co) in 2013 as a tool to inspire a life of adventure and purpose for young women.

A writer, surfer and entrepreneur, you can catch Esther riding waves or on shore eating tacos with her best friends.

Let's connect on Instagram: @estessss

For speaking inquiries (or just to be friends) contact me at: info@fearlessco.org

# FEARLESS CO.

We empower the underdogs to rise up
unhindered by fear, so that they may live
out their daring potential.

## CONNECT WITH US:

fearlessco.org

@Fearless.co_

info@fearlessco.org

Fearless Talk Podcast

F — C

# FREE E-COURSE

## THE FEARLESS GIRL
## ADVENTURES COURSE
EXPERIENCE THE JOURNEY TO FREEDOM

**6 VIDEO SESSIONS**    **4 EPIC DESTINATIONS**    **3 CRAZY CHALLENGES**    **ADVENTURE GUIDE**

Experience wild adventure as you learn a step-by-step guide on how to face your fears and achieve your dreams.

Filmed in beautiful California, enjoy breathtaking views from Yosemite, Big Sur, Pismo Beach and Huntington Beach!

Test your courage as you are challenged to face your fears head on.

The Unhindered By Fear book guides you through the course as you become fearless.

## WHAT OTHERS ARE SAYING:

"I absolutely loved your book (& E-course). I can't even begin to emphasize how much it's moved me and changed my perspective on how I'm living my life."

-McKenzie

"My goal is to be fearless for my daughter & family & myself. I struggle from PTSD after my daughters previous hospitalizations. Im slowly recognizing and trying to work through my fears to help better my life with a child who has many special needs."

-Lizzie

## GO TO: FEARLESSCO.ORG/WATCH
## FEARLESS CO.

# TAKE A FEARLESS LEAP

We are proud partners of KitePride, an anti-trafficking social enterprise located in Tel Aviv, Israel. KitePride works to eradicate modern-day slavery in an environmentally sustainable way by UPCYCLING kitesurfing sails, yacht sails, parachutes and wetsuits and turning them into handmade bags while empoying women who have been previously exploited. We believe this sustainable approach is the best solution to make a measurable differance.

We encourage you to take action against human trafficking by partnering with KitePride with us. In fact, we challenge you to give of your time and spend a few months volunteering with their team. Take a fearless leap and help others overcome their fears and achieve their dreams.

For more information go to: kitepride.com

"We live in a world that is so quick to throw away what's broken. But so often, there's a lot of treasure in what has been deemed to be trash."

Tabea Oppliger, KitePride Co-Founder

# ACHIEVE YOUR
# D R E A M S

----------

## PEN AND PAPER NEVER FORGET

USE THIS SPACE TO RECORD YOUR IDEAS, CREATE A STRATEGY,
AND HOLD YOURSELF ACCOUNTABLE TO ACHIEVING YOUR DREM.

# UNHINDERED BY FEAR

# ACHIEVE YOUR
# D R E A M S

----------

## PEN AND PAPER NEVER FORGET

USE THIS SPACE TO RECORD YOUR IDEAS, CREATE A STRATEGY,
AND HOLD YOURSELF ACCOUNTABLE TO ACHIEVING YOUR DREM.

UNHINDERED BY FEAR

# ACHIEVE YOUR
# D R E A M S
----------
## PEN AND PAPER NEVER FORGET

*USE THIS SPACE TO RECORD YOUR IDEAS, CREATE A STRATEGY,
AND HOLD YOURSELF ACCOUNTABLE TO ACHIEVING YOUR DREM.*

**UNHINDERED BY FEAR**

# ACHIEVE YOUR
# D R E A M S

----------

## PEN AND PAPER NEVER FORGET

USE THIS SPACE TO RECORD YOUR IDEAS, CREATE A STRATEGY,
AND HOLD YOURSELF ACCOUNTABLE TO ACHIEVING YOUR DREM.

# ACHIEVE YOUR
# D R E A M S
---------
## PEN AND PAPER NEVER FORGET

USE THIS SPACE TO RECORD YOUR IDEAS, CREATE A STRATEGY,
AND HOLD YOURSELF ACCOUNTABLE TO ACHIEVING YOUR DREM.

Made in the USA
Lexington, KY
10 December 2019